Of the Red Brick Building

by
RAYMOND TONY CHARLIE

Askew Creek
PUBLISHING

Published by:
Askew Creek Publishing Ltd.
9920 Cedar Street
Chemainus, British Columbia
V0R 1K1

Canadian Cataloguing in Publication Data

Charlie, Raymond Tony, 1951-
  In the Shadow of the Red Brick Building

ISBN: 978-1-9991481-1-9

1. Raymond Tony Charlie – Childhood and Youth. 2. Residential Schools. 3. Indians of North America – Cultural Assimilation. 4. Off-reserve boarding schools. 5. Indians of North America 6. Indigenous Students. 7. Kuper Island Residential School. 8. Coast Salish First Nations – Crime Against.

Editing by Warren Goulding
Front Cover Design by Constance Manning
Printed and bound in Canada by Island Blue Book Printing,
Victoria, British Columbia, Canada

Table of Contents

Foreword

It is a true honour and a privilege to be asked to write a foreword for Raymond T. Charlie's book, *In the Shadow of the Red Brick Building*. I am humbled by this work and by Raymond's courage to write it. His tender, unfettered writing style invites every reader into his story and at times you feel he is speaking directly to you. One is instantly drawn into his life story as you are invited to walk or sit alongside Raymond, to patiently listen for a while. His raw sharing of stolen childhood, innocence, struggle, pain, humour, and healing weave together a complex lifeline that touches every reader. After reading his work I found myself thinking about Raymond's words and experiences often, as if I was still immersed in his story, listening and attempting to make sense of it all. While reading, one has to wonder about the oppressive nature of humankind, specifically the cruel, formidable, and calculated actions of the Canadian government and Catholic Churches throughout its dark history. For it is painfully clear through Raymond's story that residential schools and the many other intentional actions, policies, and practices – that were designed to "kill the Indian in the Indian" – have incurred lifelong scars and dark shadows for survivors, families, communities, ancestors, and within Canada as a nation.

I was soon struck by Raymond's unspoken vulnerability that caused him to have doubts about writing this story, combined with his courageous responsibility to write it. The innate struggle to share such experiences becomes undeniably clear to readers as Raymond sheds light on his own dark shadows – along with Canada's scarred history - with relentless strength, vision, and resolve to make things better. Raymond speaks directly and openly to kindred survivors, to his family, to youth, to his ancestors, to his people, to all people, and to the future generations to come, and does so with gentle warmth and raw, honest, truth. His work is about truth, justice, healing, and hope. His compelling desire for a better future is both infectious and inspiring, calling us to listen carefully and to take action.

Raymond is also clear that this book represents his own unique and personal story while also offering a kindred connection to the thousands and millions of others who live within families, communities, nations, and the world at large. He minces no words in holding perpetrators accountable for what they have done to destroy the innocent lives of children, while holding the deeply wounded, gently, within his warm smile and embrace. It is no surprise to learn how Raymond upholds his role as Elder with such kind-hearted responsibility, integrity, support, and wisdom.

Appreciate the author's culturally masterful way of inviting you to take the time to listen carefully. Please don't read this when you are in a hurry, or when a quick read is desired, for you may not only lose its essence, you will also deny Raymond's invitation for you to sit and listen for a while.

At times you will be drawn into the mixing of past and present tenses, as well as singular and the plural. This unwitting and unique style of writing enables each reader to move seamlessly along Raymond's lifeline, as sometimes he lives the memory of each of his experiences, while other times reflecting on it. Raymond writes as he is speaking to you: enjoy this time together as you may find yourself changed from his presence.

Dr. Nadine Cruickshanks

My Invitation to You

I would like to kindly invite you to take a walk with me or perhaps have a seat next to me. I will share my journey with you; however, gently open your mind and your heart and be patient. I can talk with you, but it is easier if you just sit and listen to me for a while as my path was crammed with hardships and challenges, because I have attended two residential schools and survived. I am a survivor.

However, I am grateful as a survivor to be here, I feel so fortunate. No one may notice, but many other survivors have passed on to the spirit world, sadly, and cannot share their experiences of residential schools.

These experiences have greatly affected me, as I carried a heavy load of sad experiences with hardships that were filled with painful memories every day of my life. Even after I left these residential schools, I had flashbacks that never seemed to end and were continually a part of my life. Many of us have a silent unseen dilemma of residential school that tightly binds us in its grasp in our lives.

Initially, my experiences were very difficult for me, recalling them and reliving them in my mind. We tend to bury unpleasant experiences to try and rid the pain.

Sometimes these experiences may not necessarily be yours but may be that of a family member or friend. However, it still fills our hearts with so much pain knowing what happened to us at the residential school. It can touch us in so many ways directly or indirectly, but we have them with us constantly. We hold on to the pain and hurt in so many ways unintentionally.

I have spent many hours, days, nights and months alone capturing my thoughts and putting them into words to share here. I am a challenged writer so I am doing my utmost best here to write my thoughts and feelings to share with you.

It was not easy for me, as I had to second guess myself thinking, should I include this or how much should I share here. I wanted to be very explicit in some areas but felt I could only share so much. I tell you I almost gave up so many times; I decided to tell you how it was for me for many years, being a part of the residential school system with my experiences.

I would like to share a feeling that I have as a First Nations Elder, that makes me feel very uncomfortable. That is, we are easily criticized by many today out there across these lands who have a low opinion of our people. They continue to conceive their general thoughts of us as lazy drunks and such.

They also continue to perpetuate their feelings and views about our people. Here are my thoughts and my take on this situation. It needs to be dealt with and understood; much of this probably comes from seeing our intoxicated Indians or poor destitute ones on the street today! These souls are struggling to survive another day with so much personal hardship in their complicated lives.

I am sure many of you have no thoughts as to why it is that our people are in this state of turmoil. No one in their right mind would choose to live this way, I assure you. There are reasons for them – they suffer in their minds and bodies every day. They are at the absolute end of their rope and finding they can't do much for themselves. They become helpless and caught in their ways, destitute and struggling, usually with drug and alcohol addictions as a result.

This dire situation may be specifically related to the residential schools that were built for our people, for a duration of almost 120 years, that gave them difficulties and hardships directly or indirectly in their lives. Or perhaps it was intergenerational for them, because many families now have to deal with this across these lands and streets in Canada today.

I realize it could have easily been myself in this predicament or some of my family or relatives This dilemma continues into the lives of our people today unfortunately, with no visible end.

It's incredible for me today as I think of the two residential schools I went to with my friends. It's unbelievable though for me, as many of them are in the spirit world today, a dilemma for residential school survivors dying very young. This makes it hard for me some days, as I am still here surviving. But I have a determination that I feel I must use to help myself deal with my hardships now.

Firstly, I feel that it is important as a survivor to heal myself and become a stronger person. Also, I have had to learn that what occurred to me was not my fault. I can't accept any blame myself any longer, because I felt so much overwhelming guilt almost my entire life for what happened to me. It was the shame and guilt for what occurred that I carried deep within my heart, covering it up and hiding it.

Now I am recovering and feel stronger with a keen insight to my past experiences in my life as a survivor. Today I feel that I can use my experiences and voice to help others to understand or learn what happened to survivors who were at residential schools across Canada. I am only one person but there were 150,000 children who went through residential school experiences along with me.

Many of us attended more than one residential school; we were moved from one to another as we graduated or got older. It may help you to realize and see the many issues we have as a people today that have been brought onto us directly as a result of the residential schools we attended across Canada.

This greatly affected each of our lives because many of us had abusive encounters during our stay at these residential schools. This, of course, happened to us at a very young age. Not all students had abuse but some did.

This was one of the sad colonial actions of the Canadian government, to build residential schools and use them for our young children across Canada. Their goal was to change the child in each of us. Their primary reason was "to kill the Indian in the Indian". Our language was not permitted to be spoken and many children rarely saw their families, parents or their siblings at the residential school during the whole year.

These colonialists were basically paupers who came to these lands with colonial ways and attitudes with little regard for our peoples. They had no thought or care for our First Nations people who occupied these lands. Yet they made decisions about the lives of our people to change or destroy the ways of our life.

These residential schools they started impacted many communities and families across these lands, bringing horrid times to many children and families. Many children's lives were devastated with hardships forever because of the experiences they had as children at residential schools.

Much of it is still alive today with their government laws, regulations and various departments they continue to operate. We have lost so much as a result. This began in 1876 as their colonial government opened and ran residential schools across these beautiful lands.

I finally decided that I would no longer let myself be quiet in this role as a survivor. We suffer too much with these pains every day. It's not right for me – or those who went through these abusive situations – to suffer silently in pain. We do many things scraping by with struggles in our mind and in our hearts, not feeling very good about ourselves.

Sometimes it was difficult for me, as most days I felt dirty and not good enough to be in this world. This feeling was hard to rid of for me. Once abuse occurs to us, we feel like outcasts. These feelings remain with us, forever imbedded in our minds and hearts.

We have to live with memories that are forever in our minds and spill into our lives, reminding each one of us of our time at residential schools. It is not a good place to be. It hurts and it has given me uncomfortable restlessness.

Today I need peace and calm in my life. I want to release all pains I have; I need a good night's sleep that is restful!

My story is very personal with my thoughts and feelings that were challenging for me to write here. I had some good times but so many difficult times most of my living days. I just never felt good about myself at all. I was not happy. I was preoccupied in my thoughts most days, like I was hiding something deep inside me. It was agonizing for me to have these memories of the abuse I had at the residential schools.

Initially, my first sentences that I was able to write down were a mess, as I couldn't put very many words together. My efforts and my thoughts were coming in from everywhere as I was shakily striking letters on the keyboard. I typed pages and pages of my recollections that began very nervously; recalling them from my memories was so traumatic as I had buried them for many years, trying to ignore what happened to me as a young person.

I relived choking moments and some tearful ones too. My experiences were becoming fresh in my mind, even though they occurred decades ago at two residential schools. The hurts are still with me from all the painful times I had as a youthful teenager at these two residential schools.

I had many days full of anger and regret with countless situations, experiences that were very much like a roller coaster, with some memorable days and many disturbing ones. This space was very uneasy to be in for me as it caused me to constantly struggle in my daily activities.

Of course, one may not have noticed as it sat deep within my mind and heart. I was literally boxed in with it facing situations daily, feeling insecure as a person.

It was very unsettling to say the least and I am sure that my suffering mirrors many other survivors like myself. We become mired in the pain of our memories. Here is a glimpse into my life that spans 70-plus years, much of it challenging because of my childhood experiences.

I am a very simple man who always tries to do what I can to be honest and caring around people. I will adhere to this trait throughout my writing here. I feel that I need to write in a way that I can be completely explicit yet not offend anyone. I particularly think of all my fellow survivors at this point who remain.

I feel that I must share for the purpose of letting people know my story which may be similar to other survivors. I know we share many common feelings and experiences some days because we went to a residential school.

I am a survivor of two residential schools: Kuper Island and St. Mary's in Mission City, both in British Columbia. Kuper Island Residential School was located on what is now Penelakut Island, about a 30-minute ferry ride from Chemainus. These two residential schools have marked me for life and surely left me with mixed feelings as a result.

It is quite evident today that our story remains mostly unknown across Canada, particularly in non-Indigenous communities. Some may have a vague knowledge of residential schools. It may be shocking to read, but this is my truth and experience that I will share with you.

I am just one of those 150,000 children across Canada who attended these hellhole destroyer institutions that were set up for First Nations children. It included my late mother Lavina who attended during the 1930s, my three brothers James, Mike and Al, my three sisters Sandra, Janice and Becky. We were the second generation to attend the residential school system in our family. My aunts, uncles and many other cousins also attended during different years than myself.

It's many of their stories and experiences that helped me to move on with these writings. I continue to receive personal experiences and stories from survivors today, but for now I will share my story and experiences with you. It has consumed so much of my time and brought me so many challenges.

Throughout my writing there are photos that directly relate to what I share on these pages. They help me to tie my story together. I refer to much of my writing in terms of "we", which encompasses all survivors out there who I feel have very similar feelings or experiences as mine in some ways from their time at residential schools.

For a while, I pondered the thought of writing my story to share. It was a huge task for me because I had to face my hard times directly, which was not easy for me. My memories of abuses that I suffered at the residential schools vividly came forth. After composing myself, I finally was able to write what is here.

It took over five years working on these writings. I would type then examine my writings and make changes for more clarity. At this point, there are still many doubts for me as I have paused my writing so many times. My thoughts are that I can speak better than I can write!

I will take you through portions of my life with a glimpse into many areas of hardships I faced as a young teenager, a married man and a family man. This is as a survivor, of course, which are very specific to residential school tenure and experiences. I was so hesitant looking inward, I actually tried to write these words over a decade ago but gave up. Back then, I knew I could not admit to what I write today, as I was in a fragile state, suffering inside.

Today it is still not easy, but I will continue to lighten my load. I have found my voice that helps me to say what is written on these pages. It has helped me to reflect and share from my heart. I challenged myself to share as much as I could here. I had to think carefully about all the words I have written. They are direct, painful and sobering for me now, I can admit my abuses I suffered directly at two residential schools and in the medical system.

This is the very essence of who I am as a person today, willing to share and speak what I have experienced as it moves forward to healing myself and also educate anyone who listens to my story. I have wholeheartedly committed to stand up for, and by, my words as a survivor.

Take note, I have no need or desire to exaggerate what I say, as that won't help me or anyone. It would be detrimental to our people. So, what I write are my experiences in an honest direct way as they occurred to me in my life.

This is the way of the Elders: speak strongly, honest and direct. I am now an Elder of my tribe and now involved with other Elder groups. All the words I speak must always be honest, direct and true from my heart.

I sincerely hope by sharing with you that you can learn the journey of a survivor of residential schools and see the daily challenges that I face and deal with in my life, which spans over seven decades. This storyline of my life is basically the events of my life. I want to clear and release what I don't need in my life now.

CHAPTER 1

Breaking Families Apart

Even before Confederation, the colonizers who came to this land that would be called Canada were determined to assimilate the Indigenous peoples and get rid of what they called "the Indian problem." The government under Prime Minister John A. Macdonald, in an effort to open the West to settlement and build a national railway, undertook an oppressive policy of assimilation, confident the Indian population would eventually disappear. Residential schools would become a big part of that strategy and the first schools were run by Catholic missionaries in New France or Quebec, as it came to be called.

The federal government, with the cooperation of the Roman Catholic, Anglican and Methodist Churches, began to build churches in Ontario in the 1830s. In 1861, St. Mary's Mission Indian Residential School and Coqualeetza Indian Residential School were established in British Columbia. The first Kuper Island Residential School was opened in 1889.

I attended both Kuper Island Residential School on what is now called Penelakut Island and St. Mary's in Mission, B.C.

Eventually, 134 residential schools were built. Under the direction of the federal government, each province would build them. Then the federal government would take bids from various churches to operate the school. Normally the churches would have full control over staff and budgets. Children from ages five years and up attended the residential schools over a period of more than 100 years.

If parents protested, they could be jailed for interfering with government agents. Priests or clergy would enter villages to take children, usually under protest from families who were helpless to stop these actions. If they did attempt to resist, the RCMP could be called to assist in the removal of children. These actions directly affected the whole family including the extended family. Parents could not be in parental roles any longer, nor could the grandparents be grandparents. Losing their children greatly affected whole families and impacted the livelihood of the villages.

In some villages that were isolated, parents or grandparents could hide the children away from the priests or clergy. This was done within some families, but not all were fortunate to be in that situation to save their children. They were able to maintain their roles with a healthy First Nations child intact and have normal ties to their family, culture and language.

It's heartbreaking to think of our villages with no children, no family life or activity. Healthy families always had parents and grandparents around daily. As the children were placed into these institutions, many of them cried for their mom and dad and their siblings. Of course, it was hard for them to understand, so they went to sleep nightly, crying sadly.

I can attest to the heartbreak of a village with no children since before I attended residential school, I worked with some 30 plus junior boys who were aged six to ten years old. I was a supervisor for them at St. Mary's in Mission City in 1969. I would take them on hikes or on a run, play games, wrestle with them to no end, with hopes to burn off their energy. I sincerely felt that maybe, if they were tired, they would sleep better and quickly.

At 7 p.m., when it was bedtime for them, I would announce it was time to change into their PJs and brush their teeth. They would say good night to me and go to their beds. I walked through each section checking on them. As I would tuck many of them in, they wanted hugs. I obliged them and gave tight hugs and sent them to bed. Most times some would cry. I went over to them to check on things. "I miss my mommy" was common to hear. I would reassure them that their mom and dad missed them too and loved them. It made them feel better. Then I would tuck them under their covers, tightly. I know I wasn't their parent but my reassurance helped them to know that they were loved by their parents. No child should ever be put into this situation, being without the love and support of their parents.

No doubt all loving feelings remained for each other, but there was no family there, no hugs, no support or love at the residential school. It was a cold, stringent place and hard for many of the children. Not very many of them wanted to be there.

Today I feel that there must have been so much sadness and heartache across the lands, involving so many families and children. Many families weeping silently, thinking of their children each night, because they were separated.

CHAPTER 2

First Years at the Residential School

In 1964 we began the school year as "villagers" as the kids at the Kuper Island Residential School called us. We walked approximately one mile to the classroom section of the school every day. It was a separate building that had three classrooms for Grade 3 and Grades 4 - 6 and Grade 7. Any of those who were in higher grades were moved to Mission City, Kamloops, Port Alberni or other residential schools. This was done for decades and included our students who had to move from one residential school to another for their education.

I was in Grade 5 with about 30 other kids. They were all very friendly with me and I seemed to always get along with the young girls. Many of them would put my initials on their arm or wrist and show me they had a crush on me. I would just smile at them, which was my only response. I did get lots of love notes given to me. So innocent they were, from the young girls. The notes had titles of songs or words they identified with from the songs. I remember those girls today: Belinda, Harriet, Mary Anne, Angel and so many more. They were all great friends to me.

I sat a couple of desks behind Mary Anne who was given the nickname "Princess". In all our classwork, she ranked number one, on top of the class, and I ranked number two. It never changed during the time I was there as a student. She was very smart, with good looks as well, and a very quiet young lady most times. She had a soft, tender voice when she spoke. I liked her kind smiling face. We were good friends. I wish I could talk with her today, but she is in the spirit world now.

We would attend school as day students for the whole year with the kids who boarded at the residential school who had come from other areas. The Catholic nuns would be our teachers. We would start the day with assembly in front of the school, standing outside – rain or shine – for the raising of the flag and then the singing of O Canada. Then we would move inside to our classroom, where we would say a prayer and do a pledge to the Queen.

After that our regular program began, usually with Catechism, math, English, spelling and so on. The Catholic nuns, in their traditional black garb, sat behind their desks and taught us.

On his first day as a day student my younger brother Mike watched as a nun walked over to another boy in class, grabbed a handful of his hair, and slammed his face into the desktop. This was to discipline him and keep him in line. My brother didn't share this with me until years later. My teacher actually used a pointer stick to strike a student and broke it on him for not listening. These pointer sticks were round and made of very hard wood. Another child was grabbed by the ear and made to stand in the corner all morning for not participating in class. Many of us were in disbelief, so we tried to be attentive during class.

One of the first things that happened to me was to get a nickname. My legal middle name is Tony. Apparently, there was another Tony before I came who was called 'Tex', so I inherited the name too. I was now called "Tex" by all the other kids and for over 50 years I was known as Tex. Today, some of my friends still call me this, which is something as it brings me back over 50 years when I hear this name.

We were day students, so this was basically most of what we saw in our classrooms. None of the children uttered a word so that's the way it was left. We made many new friends and acquaintances with a lot of the kids at the school. During midday, we would break for lunch and head up to the dining room to eat with the other students.

I became very good friends with so many of the kids during this time. Many of them had autograph books. I would be asked to sign them, usually with a message or my address. I eventually bought a book myself and by year-end every page was filled with cute messages like "U R too cute to B 4 gotten," and a lot of other sayings, including some really mushy words. This was neat as I looked at it not long ago. Some 50-plus years later it's a little bit distressing for me, as many of those who signed it for me are now in the spirit world. This keepsake is so special for me as it brings me back to many of my friends who signed it and left me messages.

One of my good friends went home for the holidays to her family. After the holidays were over, she didn't return to the Kuper Island Residential School. Apparently, she drank a whole bottle of hard liquor and died of alcohol poisoning. She was only around 15 or 16 years old. She had a warm smile and wore glasses. It's obvious that she had some type of stressful encounter to do that type of reckless activity, possibly it was due to abuse or trauma. She may have witnessed an incident at the school.

It is difficult to really say, as many of the students had varying incidents of abuse that they never shared with anyone. But usually friends or acquaintances knew directly about it. I think they were afraid to share their experiences of abuses they witnessed while at the residential school.

I believe it was sometime in 1965 or 1966 that I went to the gym at the Kuper Island Residential School. When I grabbed the door handle, I changed my mind about entering. I just let go of the handle and left. I was overcome by reluctance. The same thing happened the next day. I loved to shoot basketball by myself in the gym and I did that almost every day.

Later on that day, the night watchman, my late uncle Simon, discovered the body of a young man who hanged himself on the bleachers upstairs. He had used the ropes, which were used for raising the large screen for watching movies. It was attached to large pulleys with excess rope.

Had I gone in, I would have seen the body, hanging behind the basketball hoop frame below the bleachers upstairs. So tragic it breaks my heart.

I saw another survivor recently and we spoke about this incident with the young teenager. He simply said to me, "No that is not what happened. He was a close friend of mine who was being sexually abused by Brother Kinney!" Brother Kinney was a supervisor who watched the young boys at the Kuper Island Residential School.

This friend is well into his sixties. I had seething anger with this as we both are older and can speak candidly about abuses we had at the Kuper Island Residential School.

Around 1966 I went with three other boys from Kuper Island Residential School on a trip to Williams Lake Residential School. It was during the Easter break when one of the Oblate brothers, Brian Dufour, invited me to come along with them. We stayed in a small house near the residential school there. Some children were still staying at the main building. We were asked if we wanted to ride horses. We are normally sea people but we agreed to try riding these horses. My good friend Larry Thomas and myself mounted our horses eagerly. We heard that they just came in from the range. We had no idea what that meant but they were a little wild yet as they hadn't been ridden for a while!

We grabbed the reins and gently kicked the sides of the horses to get them to move. Larry's horse bolted quickly. It was galloping fast and he was bouncing up and down. Pretty soon he was moving from side to side, struggling to stay on his horse. We were both small guys and very short so our legs just managed to reach the stirrups. I was behind laughing at the comedic sight. Luckily, he was able to stay on his horse with no injury but his horse rubbed against a fence post, ripping Larry's dress pants. Our horses kept running down the road until another rider on a horse came for us, rescuing two green riders! I was so relieved.

My close friend Lawrence was always joking and teasing everyone and he seemed constantly in conflict with the guys. Sometimes he would say, "Hi, I am Lawrence, Lawrence of Arabia!" But he was always getting under everyone's skin with his antics. He only had good thoughts it seemed, but we would always tease him back, during his talks with us.

Lawrence and I were with Dufour on this trip to Williams Lake. He also brought us to Anaheim reserve for a tour there. I remember the roads were so muddy at the time we almost got stuck there on the road. We also had a short stop at the Kamloops Residential School since Dufour had to see one of his friends there. They had a large swimming pool, I remember, that they used for skating on during the winter.

At this time I felt very fortunate to be with the other fellas, to have this outing with them. They would have been stuck at the residential school for the holidays otherwise and this got me time off the island with them, and it was a chance to see the other residential schools and accompany the other young boys.

We were out of the confines of Kuper Island Residential School and its boundaries. I was able to see a bit of their lifestyle and interests, the ranges and horses and such. But we didn't intermingle or have any conversation with them at all, at Kamloops or Williams Lake.

We are coastal people of the canoe and such, who lived from the ocean by harvests of shellfish and salmon, cod, ducks and more. We were able to get a glimpse of their style of living, with the land there. We can appreciate their ways, which are different for us to see and experience.

CHAPTER 3

Life as a Boarder: The Abuse Begins

We were all getting older, my brothers and I, so my late uncle Simon went to the residential school administration and asked if we could board there for the beginning of 1967. Just after Christmas we were admitted for the last six months of the school year. One of the first things that happened was that my hair was cut short like the rest of the boys at the school. Normally it was long, so I used hair oil to make my usual wave in my hair.

This is a picture of me when I began my first full year at Kuper Island Residential School in 1967-68 as a boarder. These were by Brylcream days. The previous year I was there for six months. It is striking to me now when I see a younger me in a photo smiling and happy. Much of this changed later as I went through days and months in the system of residential schools. I started to lose my confidence, my openness with people, and much of my happiness.

I quickly became familiar with the daily routines; brush my teeth before bed, get into PJs and into our beds. Next morning, we all headed downstairs for a shower and to get into our dress pants and shirts for the day. After that we had breakfast with all the boys in the dining room. We then went to the TV room and waited until it was time to begin classes. We would then walk almost two blocks to the little school and have assembly first with the whole school outside in front of it.

I was a very naïve youngster at the residential school. It only meant clean clothes to me and nothing else. Before attending, I also worked there at the residential school during the summer months with my brother James. We would mow the lawns, paint many rooms, do cement work by pouring sidewalks, trim the hedges, and more.

It would become monotonous for the two of us some days, then one day my brother James called to me. I went over to him to see what was up. He had a paintbrush full of paint and smacked me with it. Parts of my hair were light blue and my face, too. I was shocked he did that to me, but it took us out of the seriousness of our work.

My brother was laughing at me. It was short periods of fun and laughter with him. Our laughter must have echoed through this empty building, but we kept each other going with these antics. At the end of the summer our hair had different colours of paint throughout.

With just the two of us in this huge school building, James always found a way to have fun, mostly at the expense of myself. We never argued or fought with each other and we had a great sibling relationship with each other. One day we were moving cement bags. They were around 70 pounds each. Of course, we had to see who could carry more and I edged him by one bag. Not often this would occur because he is generally known as the tough guy. He is the tough one, no matter what he does.

All summer long my brother and I worked in this large empty building, ignorant of what was happening to the children who boarded at this place. I remained clueless at this point about what occurred behind these walls with the children there. My brother James and I were not directly affected at all by abuse at the residential school during this period.

During our second summer, four young teenage girls worked there and would cook lunch for us. I remember Doreen, Irene and Valerie but the other name slips my mind at this time. They were from the Interior of B.C. They worked during the summer cleaning around the kitchen and other areas of the school.

Periodically, some of the fellas would share with me sad stories or history during their time there, usually in a gentle, somber, quiet soft tone, and in confidence, of course. I was shown a huge steel bin incinerator situated at the far end of the soccer field. I was told of the newborn babies that were tossed into it. These babies were born to the young girls at the residential school.

They also showed me the apple tree where some babies were buried beneath. Another area that was known was behind the old barn, which was later converted into a gymnasium. Babies were also buried there. So incredible what our young girls went through at Kuper Island Residential School. So heartbreaking to share this now.

I was brought along on a run to Mary's Point (along the seashore) and told of two young ones who found a log they would use to try and swim to get to Chemainus so they could go home to their families. But they drowned. This information was in fact true, as it was confirmed by my cousin Richard. This run usually continued along the bluffs to the steep cliffs, which is a beautiful scenic area. The small town of Chemainus is viewed directly across the way. I ran this occasionally, about a mile and a half each way.

I knew some of the fellas would pick apples there at Mary's Point, and store them for snacks, probably because some days they were still hungry. They would lift the bottom of their shirts, roll it up into a pocket for apples from the tree and eat them later. One day one of the boys gave an apple to me. It was huge and green. I took a bite from it and noticed that it wasn't even sweet or good tasting at all for regular eating.

Perhaps one of the most challenging days for me was getting on the old St. Louis boat, a cargo boat used to transport food supplies to the residential school, with five other students. We were scheduled for dental treatment. I will never forget this day as long as I live. We were all just happy to get off the Island and get time out of class for the day.

We arrived in Chemainus, got off the boat and then walked up to the panel wagon for our shuttle to Ladysmith, where we would see the dentist. We arrived at the office and waited outside together on chairs. Strangely we didn't talk to each other or say a single word. Now that I think about it, maybe their silence meant they knew something about the dentist.

My turn finally came. The dentist said to me after my examination, "you look like a tough guy, so I won't need any freezing for you!" I had no idea what that meant but soon learned. While I sat there he began drilling my teeth for three fillings. Without freezing on my gums! It was one of the most painful ordeals for me as I pushed my head back into the headrest, closing my eyes. I could feel tears begin to form and fall down the sides of my face from the intense pain. Each moment felt like minutes to me.

I would open my eyes and could see smoke rising from the drill in front of me. It was so painful as I never had dental treatment before. It was like toothaches piled one upon the other with no end. I was a very rigid young patient lying there stiff as a board in the dental chair, with no options available for this treatment. The old dental drills were not like today's, using water to assist with drilling. Eventually it was over, but my mouth was very sore and my gums swollen.

Thankfully that was my only trip to this old dentist who got away with abusing us with his dental treatment because he didn't freeze our gums at all. He was a very old man with no conscience at all for this dental work or how it was for his patients.

This was a common experience for a lot of our survivors to go through. Regularly, men who were practicing to become dentists would come to the residential school to treat children.

Fortunately, I still have most of my teeth in my mouth; periodically I still get triggers, though, when going to a dentist, so I share my experience with them. They are very receptive and make sure that I don't have any pain during my treatment.

However, I find that when I sit on these dental chairs today, I usually find myself clenching the arms of the chair or pinching my thumb against my finger in case I get pain. This remains fresh in me today, some 50 plus years later. I am very grateful for my dentist, Dr. Levin, who has been so considerate and kind with his treatment to me. He always checks with me, asking if I feel pain and offers to add more freezing to my gums. He completely puts me at ease now during his work on my teeth. I have so much respect for him and his considerate staff.

As I became a part of the residential school I began short sessions with team sports, such as basketball, and volleyball, so we made a trip to Christie Residential School on Meares Island. We had a brief stop at Port Alberni Residential School first. I had desires for team sports but I was not talented for any of them. There was also soccer for the guys but I had no abilities to kick the ball. Besides, the soccer boots were very old and had bars beneath them. They weren't very comfortable and the front of the shoes were all round and hard, too, like steel.

Frequently, I heard disturbing incidents of the young intermediate boys who were sniffing gas from the old GMC or Pontiac parked by the workshop. It was parked behind the boys' side of the school. Apparently, they would just take off the cap and sniff. The gas cap was on the unseen part of the old pickup so they could stand by the truck and no one would see them. They would get high from this activity.

Many of these boys were pre-teen. Now when I think about it, maybe they were looking for an escape. Probably from abuse and looking for a way to forget the experiences they had to deal with. So incredible to write this now. It is sad to recall this memory about the young boys who did this while at the Kuper Island Residential School.

There weren't very many of us during this time. Clyde, Tweedy, Alec, Felix and others, but my mind goes blank for the rest of the young fellas. We had a low number at this time as most of the older boys were moved to other schools.

Initially, Brian Dufour, had some funds to take two boys to Expo 67 in Montreal. They backed out so he asked my brother James and myself to go in their place. In the fall of 1966 we agreed to go as both of us were just getting involved in the band just after Christmas. It was a drum and fife band. I started out in a flag-bearer spot. Later, I was given the bass drum to play.

We marched in local parades and prepared for the bigger one in Victoria called the Victoria Day Parade. It had other musical bands, clowns, and more. It was a huge parade for us. It would take almost two hours to march the whole route.

This was the parade celebrating Queen Victoria. Somewhere during this time Brother Brian Dufour had done a radio interview. His story was picked up by the Victoria newspaper about our trip to Montreal for Expo 67. Somehow, discussion began as to why not take the whole marching band from the residential school. The government gave a grant to assist. Word got out to the public about the trip and soon pledges were coming in to assist to make the trip a reality. A school in Victoria also began to fundraise for our school band trip.

The school was called S.J. Willis. They did a great job helping with the fundraising and today I am very thankful to them for their efforts to assist us to make the trip to Montreal. The whole school helped out, donating their time for fundraising for us.

Soon, enough money was raised for the band's flight. There were about 32 in total who played in our band, plus support staff. Word also got out to the International Clubs of Canada based in Montreal. It was a collection of the Lions Club, Rotary and other clubs across Canada who came forth and paid for our accommodations in Montreal. The generosity of many groups and agencies shared with us is not forgotten. I thank you.

Throughout the spring weather the school band continued to practise every day. We would march and play on the soccer field adjacent to the school. Also, we did a lot of performances for the public locally. We even had time to have a portrait of the school band together and I believe the Victoria newspaper photographers took our picture. Soon school was finished and in June our group packed our bags and instruments for our trip east to Montreal Expo 67.

None of us had ever been on an airplane before. We began our trip on an old DC3 out of Nanaimo for a fight to Vancouver. It took off shaking and rattling and the propellers were loud, but it still brought smiles to everyone on board. Everyone looked so neat. The girls had light blue dress suits with skirts and the boys had on grey dress pants with white shirts and ties with a dark blue blazer.

We waited patiently for our flight to Montreal at the Vancouver Airport. Finally, our group was called and we were seated. The jet took off but before too long many of the band members began to get motion sickness. It spread to many of the group pretty quick. Many began to barf into the handy bags in front of them. Luckily it didn't affect me.

During the flight, the captain did announcements about land sites all across Canada. We were all invited to view the flight deck individually with the pilot and co-pilot, a treat for us to view their area firsthand along with instruments and such. It was nice to see smiley faces walking down the aisle with the stewardesses to the front.

Once we arrived in Montreal, the group was excited as we were in a huge city. We had to tidy ourselves in our dress suits because an invitation came in from Mayor Jean Drapeau at City Hall. He welcomed us to the city and spoke to the band. We were asked to sign the large gold book that all dignitaries who came to the city signed. We had a blind middle-aged tour guide who escorted us with his dog. He knew so much about all the attractions of the city. We even visited a large cathedral on Mount Royal.

We were taken to all the exhibits and given a tour of the exposition called Man and His World and we viewed all the architecture of the huge buildings. I gave an interview to a *Montreal Gazette* reporter after one of our performances. My shoulders were actually being massaged during the time. As it was windy marching along the St. Lawrence River that day, my bass drum was like a sail blowing me along. It was pretty easy, as I weighed only around 100 pounds. I had marks on my shoulders from the straps on the drum. A picture was also taken for the *Montreal Gazette*. It was hot and humid with over 300,000 people in attendance.

Most of the beautiful exhibits were on an island in the middle of the St. Lawrence River. We had tours of all the exhibits over two days when we weren't marching and playing our instruments.

We had another performance to do. The Queen was there that day but she was on the Monorail for her visit. Thankfully our uniforms were red with vests and chaps, which was great for our stay and performances. They were light and cooler for us as previous uniforms were pretty traditional, all white with a white cap. These new uniforms were custom made by seamstresses at the residential school. They were like Indian style and very attractive to wear. They looked smart on the whole school band.

We had another three empty days there so the International Clubs purchased a stay for us at the summer camp. It had canoeing, archery, swimming and other activities. We enjoyed ourselves together, just a bunch of kids having fun. It went by very quickly. Then we had to head back to our motel and get into our dress suits.

A dinner banquet was planned and hosted by the International Clubs in our honour for the last evening in Montreal. It was in a large hall with 200 to 300 club members present. We had some tables set up for the band and chaperones to sit together. Everyone was happy and smiling as we had never had a dinner with full silverware setup before. Halfway through the dinner our supervisor, Brother Dufour, came over and asked me to thank the Club members, a surprise for me. I grabbed a napkin and began to write a short speech of thanks to them. As we soon finished eating our desserts I stood up and gave my speech of thanks. It went well and the club members clapped after I spoke.

They were very gratified to hear we had a good time and we were thankful to them for our accommodation and time at the summer camp. The group then headed to our motel for the last night in Montreal.

The next day, all bags were packed as everyone began to load their luggage. On the bus after breakfast, Dufour came over to my brother James and myself. He said, "Keep your bags, you will be staying with me for a while." We were surprised to hear that.

We said goodbye to the whole band and everyone lined up and gave us hugs. Some cried as we knew we would not see each other again as they had finished their time at the residential school. They all got on the shuttle and left while three of us watched them and waved goodbye.

We got into a cab and headed to Brian Dufour's parents' home. They lived at Greenfield Park which is a suburb of Montreal. We met his parents and chatted briefly and then we were led to a couple of rooms downstairs where we would be staying for our visit. There was a hide-a-bed in a small living area and a single bedroom. The first night I stayed in the small bedroom and my brother James was with Dufour on the hide-a-bed. The next day we toured Montreal a bit and drove by the Forum. Then we went to Quebec City.

Later, Dufour took us to Cornwall and Hamilton to visit his sister and brother and their families. They worked at Stelco, the huge steel company in Hamilton which was known as the Steel City. We had dinner together that night and were introduced to a game called Ouija. We had fun playing that with their whole family. Again, we had an area set up for sleeping in the basement.

Dufour's sister came over and hugged me tight. I was surprised when she said, "We would like to adopt you!" I just smiled and said I would think about it. The same thing happened at Dufour's parents' home, as they said the exact thing to me. I had no idea where that offer came from, but really I thought, "I have family back home in B.C. I can't leave them. I wouldn't think of moving anywhere else."

After breakfast we drove down to Lake Erie, to a racetrack, which was a first for us. We were pretty young, but brother James said, "I like that horse" as they were led by their handlers. He went to the ticket booth and bet two dollars. The race began so we watched with great interest. Surprisingly, his horse placed so he brought his ticket back to the booth and cashed it, winning $16. After the race, we headed to Niagara Falls. It was a treat for us walking along the famous sight-seeing area. We went beneath the falls where it was so loud and you could feel it, but we enjoyed it. I particularly loved the Canadian side with the water coming over the falls. The American side had lots of rocks beneath it.

After spending time at the Falls it was decided to go into New York State, just on the other side of the bridge between the U.S. and Canada. We had dinner at an Italian restaurant which was a treat for us. There was excitement in the air as the Beatles were coming to America and they were visiting Buffalo, I believe.

That night when we arrived back at the Dufour home, I slept with Dufour on the hide-a-bed. The next morning my brother James said, "Did he do any anything funny with you?" I silently nodded "yes" as we were usually around people, so I could not say anything.

Dufour knew someone in the Air Force so he told us we were going to the Air Force base. He drove for a while until we arrived and got out of the vehicle. We had no clue but he had arranged for us to ride in the Goodyear Blimp. The engines were running and it was loud. We walked up some portable stairs and got inside the huge cabin beneath the Blimp. It had around four crew on board including the captain and co-pilot and it took about 12 passengers.

Eventually the ropes were released by the ground crew and the engines began to rev loudly. We soon began to ascend into the sky, airborne two or three thousand feet up, so we had a tour of Montreal from the sky. At one point the pilot did a dive for us. The passengers were all smiles including my brother James and myself. In no time the tour was over and we would land back at the base. We then headed back to the Dufour residence.

Most days we would sit on the stairs in front of the house because it was so hot and humid. We could hear a clanging noise so we investigated it. Over to the side and the end of the street below the trees, four men were playing a game of horseshoes. My brother James and I played this game too, and loved it.

We watched them play their game. They spoke French to us asking if we played this game. Luckily one of the fellas was Italian but could speak English. Thank goodness. He asked if we played and we nodded "yes we do," so we joined the game with them. At least we had some fun now, having something for us to do other than sitting on the stairs.

Dufour had left us with his parents as he went visiting. But these men enjoyed our company with lots of laughter and jabbering. They even showed us where they stored the horseshoes so we could play it anytime. It was pretty handy for us to kill time together. It kept us busy as we had nothing else to do.

This was actually the most time I ever had with my younger brother James. For that reason I am thankful today. We had almost every minute with the two of us hanging out together, for all our activities over the summer.

The FLQ, a militant separatist group that was active in Quebec at that time, was bombing a lot of mailboxes not far from where we stayed so we never ventured far from the Dufour residence. We just stayed at the home all the time.

To this day, some 50 plus years later, I have never really spoken to my brother James about the summer in Montreal. Maybe someday we may have a chance to reflect on our time there. Playing in the band, traveling, staying in Greenfield Park for the summer, and touring all the locales.

We had so much time together as we hardly saw Brian Dufour. Most of the time we were there at his parents' home. Surprisingly, we never watched TV either. James and I had so much time together. But after that summer, we would rarely see each other.

After that summer we spent with Dufour, he quit his role as a brother with the Catholic Oblate faith. A few years later, I received a phone call from the RCMP from Toronto and I gave disclosure of sex abuse by Dufour at his parents' home in Montreal. They were going to fly me in to testify against Dufour and I agreed I would be available.

A short time later, I received another call from the RCMP stating the case against Dufour would be cancelled. Apparently, Dufour was jailed for abusing children that he was caring for in a foster home. He died while he was imprisoned. I was not given details so I didn't push for any information.

CHAPTER 4

First Full Year as a Residential School Boarder: The Abuse Escalates

In the beginning of September 1967, I started my first full year as a boarder at the Kuper Island Residential School. I was assigned to the senior dorm with the other young teenagers. We were on the top floor on the boys' side of the school. It was all set up in cubicles with tiny individual rooms with bunk beds for two. I had stayed there only one night when my supervisor, Glen Doughty said, "You are now assigned to the room before the entrance to the dorm".

I packed my belongings and moved there and met my new roommate Felix. A young fella around my age, he wore black-rimmed glasses. He had curly black hair and was about my size but on the lean side. Even though we became friends, we didn't get close, but I feel none of us really did. Our conversations were very basic, but I didn't give it any thought nor pushed our relationship. I was more outgoing, I suppose, more talkative and such, but we were friends.

Felix was given the nickname "Professor" because of his glasses. Almost everyone in the residential school had a nickname that they were known by such as Tweedy, Shy Blossom, Bubbles, Princess, Chimo, Angel, and so on. Some days I think about most of them and wonder how they are and if they are still alive. I became very close to some of them, especially the girls. I visited many of them when I was a day student, when there were no restrictions for me at all. We had a lot of volleyball and tetherball outside during the good weather. Some days I would sit there at a picnic table chatting with them. These were great innocent times with many of them, talking about basic stuff, music, friends and acquaintances we had together. They used to tease me a lot, jokingly, we had a lot of laughs together, Angel, Belinda and other young girls.

I stayed in that tiny room with two single beds in it, with Felix, for two or three weeks before I was moved by my supervisor, Doughty. He said, "We have lots of room, so I am giving you your own room."

It was past the boys' large bathroom. There were two small bedrooms down there with another single bathroom at the far end of the floor. I again gathered my things and moved. This room was about 10 feet x 10 feet with a door and two large windows and a sink. There was only a bunk bed for me, so I used the lower bed.

One evening, Doughty came to see me and said, "I think we should get to know each other, so you are invited to my room this evening!" I simply said, "Sure." I had no second thoughts of this man when he looked at you with those thick, dark rimmed glasses. He always smiled. It was almost devious because it was a teeth smile. It wasn't a smiley face smile.

I had no doubts about him at the time as he was always nice to me. He had been my supervisor for a little over two weeks at the time. He was about 5'10," weighing about 170 pounds and always wore his dark robe similar to a priest, all black. When one sees this type of dress, you think, this is a man of God. Sometimes he carried a Bible with him.

I had never been to his room before as it was just below the senior boys' dorm. It had a desk, a chair and a double bed in it with two large windows on the third floor facing the waterfront. Almost over the front entrance of the building, there was another bedroom next to his room. On the other side of it was the infirmary for the boys who got sick or needed medical attention. I sat on the chair and chatted with him briefly. All small talk. He said, "It's getting late, come here and lay down." He had his bedside lamp on. I was laying there ready to sleep with this man!

At this time, I hadn't given any thought for me being there with him alone. I was a gullible young teenager thinking this was a visit with him. There were no guarded feelings or alarms for me at this time. I was just a naïve and trusting young person!

He turned off his bed lamp then moved close to me, putting his hand in my pajamas grabbing my penis. I could almost feel my eyes pop in the dark. I couldn't breathe as I held my breath. I was literally beside myself with disbelief. I was shocked. This had occurred once before with Dufour on our trip to Quebec. He fondled me to ejaculation, and I lay there in wet pajamas. He then grabbed my hand and put it on his penis. "Rub it," were his only words to me. Still in shock I did his bidding.

Later I lay there in silence. I could not sleep or close my eyes. I lay there feeling violated. I had no more trust and was feeling confused. I felt crazy lying there in bed with this man. Early the next morning I headed to my room in a very tired state with a numb feeling in my head. I was in total disbelief for what I just experienced with this man!

I was becoming so very uncomfortable, becoming more guarded and isolated, not really trusting this man. I did what was necessary, going through the daily routines along with the other fellas.

My demeanor as a youth began to change. I was more serious and slowly losing confidence in myself. I had so much uncertainty and puzzlement at this time, wishing I could be done with Doughty.

Little did I know that Doughty had me lined up for further encounters, with his twisted abusive way with me. One night, as I was sleeping on the bottom of my bunk bed in the darkness, I was abruptly awakened from my sleep by Doughty. He grabbed my head and pushed his penis into my mouth. He pumped to ejaculation, got off his knees and left my room. I lay there gagging from this violation. He did this to me again and again over the course of four months, always waking me from my sleep to satisfy himself sexually.

It was so sickening to experience this with him. It was very difficult to get a peaceful sleep for many endless nights. It seemed that when I did fall asleep, he got to my room to awaken me. These encounters were becoming hard to deal with. I had to contend with this continual helpless feeling nightly.

Today, this is still my sleep pattern, very irregular and unrested. I now have an innate dislike for dark rooms. It was a mental thing or trigger that affected me for over 50 years because of Doughty's sex abuse of me. Darkness seemed OK but dark rooms were the hardest for me to accept.

Strikingly memorable and uneasy for decades to contend with, it was, for me, a quiet battle to continually fight in my mind. I could not deal with it but struggled with this silent battle in my mind. It seemed impossible to find a peaceful rest and sleep.

Finally, one night in December, as it was bedtime, I thought to myself, "I am going to move to the top bunk tonight." I climbed to the top and just slept. Doughty may have come to my room but he never bothered me again. I was at least able to sleep regularly. I never shared or spoke a word to any of the other fellas about this at all. It became my burdensome secret of shame that I harboured my whole life!

Perhaps Doughty may have begun to abuse another boy after he finished with me. He was just a deviant, out to satisfy his sick needs. I learned later he was a twisted abuser hiding behind a religious position.

Unfortunately for me, someone posted information online that Mary passed to the spirit world. She will always hold a special place in my heart, as she was so genuinely warm and caring to me. I will always cherish my memories, this warm sweet lady.

Violation is disrespectful and controlling and can send wrong messages to some who are so vulnerable. I hid these violations deep inside my thoughts and memories. It was so troublesome to do because of immense shame. There are no avenues for a victim, except eternal struggles with silence.

I think this is a trait that survivors take onto themselves. It is the shame that we have which stops us from sharing with anyone. Silence seems to be characteristic for us. The shame was me keeping quiet, even though it hurt. No doubt it was a helpless feeling for me to live with at the time, especially with an authority figure as the culprit. Perhaps it was fear that kept me this way, harbouring my abuse and abuser.

This definitely affected me around all my young girl friends. We remained close friends, but I had no thoughts of building a girlfriend relationship, even though I thought of it sometimes. I had absolutely no confidence in myself. It seemed my desires were overridden by the abuse I was suffering from. Thankfully, I remained just friends with them all, no expectations, only friendship.

As I moved through my teen years, I questioned myself constantly, wondering to myself: would I be a homosexual man because of the sexual abuse from two men when I was young? Their violations were haunting to me. I had doubts and questioned myself. Even though many young girls made overtures to me wanting to begin a boy/girlfriend relationship, my youthful insecurity within myself was overwhelming. I was not confident with myself to kiss and hug or do all the mushy stuff youth do together.

I did have crushes myself, with these pretty young girls a lot of times. And so their cute love notes would come to me a lot. But I made no effort to start anything with them. Perhaps it was the safest move for me during that time period of my life.

I feel that being young and clueless about these abusers sets us up for abuse. We didn't look for these men; they found us since we were so young and naïve. When this happens to us, we become part of this chaotic abuse system that was so rampant at residential schools.

My nature has always been to be very kind and accepting of anyone. I feel this is also why Doughty took advantage of me. I had absolutely no rough edges in my make-up and this made me vulnerable. I was manipulated in so many ways so he could take advantage of me. I can clearly see that when I look back at myself during my time at the Kuper Island Residential School.

CHAPTER 5

Our Move to St. Mary's Residential School

At the end of the 1968 school year, preparations were made to move me and my siblings to St. Mary's Residential School in Mission City. I was placed with the senior boys, all mid-teens and older. The students were from various places such as the Fraser Valley, Sechelt, Mt. Currie, the Interior, Vancouver Island and more.

There were about fifty or sixty senior guys in different grades, but we stayed at the residential school in Mission City while attending the public high school. There were intermediates and junior children as well.

Here I am with brother James, one of three younger brothers who is 14 months younger than me. We are standing in front of the girl's side of the residential school at St. Mary's Residential School. I am on the left and James is on the right. I had asked him to be in a picture with me as we just started our time at the school in Mission. James was always more outgoing and involved in sports, especially soccer.

My younger sister Janice and myself outside the entrance of St. Mary's Residential School. She is my middle sister of three sisters.

I only went for my Grade 9 and 10 at Mission High School, where we would be bused every day to school. So crazy though, I feel, as almost all our people would be shuffled into occupational classes immediately. They tried to place me there, too, but I said, "No, I want to be put into a regular academic class."

It was actually kind of neat, as for once I would be in the same residential school as siblings, Sandra, Janice, Mike and James. I saw my older sister Sandra frequently as she played in the school band and on the senior basketball team at St. Mary's. She would practise basketball and invite me to scrimmage with them. Sandra had lots of friends and was so talented playing the snare drum in the St. Mary's band. She was the only sibling I saw quite often. It was a welcome change for me to associate with my sister regularly.

I had a memorable moment my first night. After brushing my teeth, I walked over to my bed, pulled over the top blanket covers to lie down, trying to cover up. I couldn't do it because one of the fellas did a French sheet on my bed, which was folding the top sheet in half to make it look like two sheets. When I got back up from my bed, about ten of the older boys were laughing at me as I struggled to get under the bed covers. This was my welcome to St. Mary's Residential School. I met Bruce, Elvis, Cecil, Ralph Martin, Earl, Arthur and tons of other fellas.

I still wasn't blessed with skills to play soccer or basketball at St. Mary's but I tried to play when I could during their practices. It was neat as one of the fellas said, "you are old enough to join the army reserves." So, I figured I might as well try it.

We would practise marching together during the week at Abbotsford. We got uniforms that we had to dress in for the evenings, then had sessions about firearms with army surplus rifles. We learned how to take them apart and clean the parts and reassemble them.

Some weekends we would go to the army base at Chilliwack to practice firing our rifles. I was able to hit the target at 350 yards. We also learned how to use the rocket launchers, called a bazooka. Bren guns were on tripods that could be fired on automatic and rapidly. We learned how to throw hand grenades. It was neat to get away from St. Mary's to enjoy these new experiences and eat with the regular forces.

We had some marches with simulated wars and such. It was challenging going through all the regular routines that the army men did, especially learning to maneuver in the dark and having to go through underground mazes in the darkness. I was behind one fella in one section, turning in a small area in the maze, when he moved his boot and got me right on the nose. When I exited the maze, guys came running over to me because I was covered in blood on my face and army fatigues.

As I became acquainted with the other young people from the Mainland and other areas around Vancouver Island, I made new friends with them all. It was announced that we would have a skit night, so along with two friends I tried a comedy skit. We got some laughs so that was great for us, even though it was scary to get up in front of friends to do this performance.

In a month or so we had a pie-eating contest along with some other indoor activities in the gymnasium. I picked a young friend, Judy S. to help me with mine. I was on all fours on the floor, directly above a beautiful cherry pie, homemade of course. I never thought about it, but the floor was covered with newspapers where the pies were and my young friend was across from me blindfolded.

A signal was given and she then had to dig into the pie with her hands while blindfolded to feed me the pie. Everyone was watching and laughing, as our partners had to find our mouths and put pie into it. Sometimes she missed my mouth and was rubbing it into my face. It must have been a riot to watch. I didn't place at all but had some great pie and had lots of it on my face, hair, eyebrows, on my nose and even in my ears.

Every other month we would have sock hops in the dining room when all the tables and chairs were pushed aside. A record player was set up with speakers and everyone used to bring their 45 rpm records to play. Usually, most of the lights were turned off. My cousin Lewis and I would volunteer to play the records for the dance. Occasionally I would get up and dance and have fun with the rest of the teens.

I always loved to jog and run three to five miles every day at the residential school with my good friend Mel. It was one of the only activities I could do well. We ran in the rain, snow and sometimes the sunny weather. My running was always hampered though by some sea urchin spines in my left foot. When I was 13 years old, I went out fishing with my cousins. We stopped at a reef and I got off the boat, slipped on kelp and slid into a crevice on the reef. It was full of sea urchins and I stepped on one with my left foot. It was impaled with spines. Today I still have five of them in my left foot.

St. Mary's was well known for its girls' marching band. My older sister Sandra played the snare drum in this band beautifully. They had great songs and routines and were so adept and professional as a group.

In 1970 it changed and became a mixed band, so I joined and signed up to play the bass drum. The instructor worked with me so I learned the beat. One day he grabbed my drumstick and said the beat must be constant and quick. We marched the whole day at the army base in Chilliwack and after two hours my gauntlet was full of pus as I got blisters that broke inside. I could feel anxiety from this practice but was determined to do the best I could. I played the drum for the whole second year at St. Mary's Residential School.

One thing that was so different for me was that in the evenings we were given snacks. Usually, a couple of guys would take a trolley to the kitchen and load it up with loaves of bread. It would be accompanied with large bucket containers of peanut butter and jam while other times it would be salmon mixed with onions and mayonnaise in a large bowl. We also had orange juice or lemonade for drinks before bedtime.

One evening, after supper, all the seniors were in the TV room watching Montreal play hockey against Chicago. It was an exciting game and all the chairs were set up in front of the TV in the recreation room. The lights were turned off so it was dark in there. It was an engrossing game for us all. I sat in the very front of the group with my feet propped up, just loving the game and cheering on Montreal.

All the guys were yelling and screaming at the TV and I was soaking up the game with the play of Worsley, Cournoyer, Savard, Mahovlich, Richard, Beliveau and all the Montreal greats. Being in the very front of the TV, I was immersed in the game and not really aware of anything happening around me.

Suddenly I just heard a voice in the dim lit room amidst the TV glow. "What are you doing here?" I just turned to look and was punched so hard I was knocked to the floor. I was dazed, on my knees and hands with my head spinning. As I looked up I was back handed very hard on the side of my face. My head turned from the slap and I could see I was the only one in the room. All the rows of chairs that were behind me were now empty. It was Brother Francis. He was a balding middle-aged brother, who had previously been at Sechelt Residential School, I believe. He was my supervisor. He then yelled, "Get up!" I was still groggy. When I stood up, he pushed me forward. "Get to my office," he screamed.

As I walked into his office, he went to his desk where he opened a drawer. Pulling out a strap he said, "Put up your arms, you are getting 10 straps on each arm!" I put them up in disbelief and was hit on the forearms with this strap that was 18" x 2.5" inches wide. Initially the strapping stung as he used it like a whip. My forearms and hands were beginning to get hot. They then became numb. As he finished, he yelled loudly, "get to study!" I walked over to my cupboard and tried to grab my books but couldn't because my hands and fingers were useless. They weren't able to move from the strapping.

My eyes were tearing from the pain. Thankfully one of the fellas was there next to the TV room so I asked him to tuck my books under my arm. Then I walked to the study room, where all the guys were at the tables, studying quietly with their books. I just sat for the duration of study since I couldn't turn the pages of my books.

My arms, down to my hands and fingers, were frozen for over six hours before I could use them at all. They were still very sore, paralyzed and burning from the strapping I received.

To this day, it is hard to believe that I hadn't done anything wrong. I had no infractions at all, but I was severely punished by this Catholic brother for being late for study. My hands and arms remained in a painful state for some time. I couldn't even use the bathroom.

I felt the bruises for days until they healed. I had to wear long sleeved shirts to hide my dark bruised arms, so no one could see them.

I feel now that he was mentally unstable for what he did to me. I hadn't heard of anyone else getting strapped by Francis, or they never told anyone. I wasn't stealing, fighting or anything but was severely punished by being punched, slapped and strapped. This was in the fall of 1969, I believe, but it remains fresh in my mind today. I can still see the bald-headed brother looking at me through his rimless glasses with his piercing big, grey eyes. This memory still impacts me today.

I had no intention of skipping out on our nightly study session that evening. I feel the fellas probably thought they were pulling a joke on me for not telling me that it was time for study. I can't blame them.

This was my last experience with abuse. They all were traumatic times for me: dental work without freezing, sex abuse, and physical abuse. The most difficult one for me was the sex abuse, which has impacted me for my whole life. These memories I tried to forget, but it's impossible to erase from my mind and heart.

There is absolutely no way that could be done. We are not geared to let it go. Many of us continue to live with it every day and try to bury it. Sex abuse goes to the very core of us because it was dominating, overpowering and made me feel helpless with defeat. These events are huge and are forever imprinted in my memories.

I held these abuses in the back of my mind, ignoring them. I pushed myself to get through each day the best I could. It kept me in a serious, quiet state most days. It was a pretty sad way for a young man to be. Absolutely no one should be put into a frame of mind like this.

Some of my friends or acquaintances also had some horrid experiences as students, including having their teeth removed for no reason. My late friend, Bill, had his sister pushed off a fire escape, three floors up, murdered by a nun during the 1930s or '40s.

There were countless acts of sexual abuse by priests, nuns, brothers and staff. It hurts to write them now, but these were acts of extreme abuse. I feel they have to be discussed so closure can occur for our families who had this happen to their family members. Especially the suicides that happened across Canada, as our people wanted to end their painful memories.

It is so traumatic for anyone in this mode, suffering from abuse at the residential schools.

CHAPTER 6

The Charlie Family's Experience

My mother, Lavina, was a residential school survivor of the 1930s. She was a petite woman with long hair that was very black, thick and curly. She was a very slender woman of 5'2", tiny with a big heart. She loved to laugh when she was around family, one of those neat qualities I remember so much.

Even though she passed away some 55-plus years ago, I wondered why she had those striking features. Our family has some Hawaiian ancestry as told to me by my late aunt.

My late mother Lavina and her younger sister Ramona were full-time residential school students. They rarely left the place at all. She and my aunt Mona were both fluent in our language, but my mother did not teach us. I feel the reason is that they were punished harshly for speaking our Hul'qumi'num language during her time. Today I am torn because I can't speak it. I understand some words but can't speak my language.

During my mother's time, the students who spoke their language in residential schools were punished. They had to wash their mouths out with soap, were made to do cleaning, or were not given food during mealtimes. Some were beaten for speaking their own language, even though it was all they could speak!

I spoke with an Elder who shared that when he got to the residential school, he only spoke our Hul'qumi'num language. He was talking to another young boy in class when the Catholic nun came over and grabbed him by both ears, harshly, yanking them. He was forced into the closet because he was not speaking English. He could not speak it but was still punished for it. Sadly, he just needed to go to the washroom and was asking the young boy for directions. This beautiful man recently passed on to the spirit world and will be missed in our communities. He was also an Elder in our First Nations court system with me. (He gave me permission to share this incident involving the evil nun)

Today it is clear that many of my mother's generation had much trauma in their lives. She died at a very young age, unfortunately, leaving my brothers and sisters motherless at an important time in our lives. I had just turned 13 when she passed and for many years I had a void in my life. In many ways this void was filled by my aunts Mary and Ramona, who shared guidance and love with support that helped me to become who I am today. I am very grateful to them both.

My late mother, Lavina, who attended residential school in the 1930s at Kuper Island. She was a beautiful woman who always held us when she was near us and she was a very resourceful woman who loved us, as a mother, when she was around us as a parent.

My children were deprived of a grandmother that they needed, like all children in this world. The loving embrace from a grandma is important. It is usually special times for sure. Grandmothers are always the patient teacher in families, giving stability, with love and patience and insight to grandchildren.

I would have loved for my three sons to know her smile, laughter and love. This breaks my heart just to write this. It's unfair to my family with her absence today; the effects of being a survivor, seeing your mother dying so young with unfinished loving duties.

My parents were very traditional in the 1950s. My late dad Jim hunted and harvested seafood, feeding us clams, ducks, and deer meat from areas around our reserve. My mother was a knitter of Cowichan sweaters. She would knit for 18 or 20 hours straight on a sweater, finish it, then wash it. It was an amazing feat to knit a whole sweater in that time period. Her needles were always clicking as she sat making a sweater out of wool. My late dad usually helped with the sleeves and any excess wool remaining was used to make toques, socks, or mittens. She was a beautiful knitter of all these items. It was high quality knitting of course, as she took pride in her work. Not very many people hired Indians in the early 1950s, so knitting was the only source of income for the family.

My late mother Lavina passed to the spirit world in 1964. So grateful that one of my Penelakut family, late Verneda, gave me this picture which was over 70 years old. It was very special to me to see this picture.

Our parents managed to bring us up during these challenging days of the early 1950s. I remember that periodically we would receive commodities from the government. It was distributed to our reserve, which was, of course very helpful to our family. I remember the Spam, flour, Pilot biscuits, and powdered milk. Sometimes even a large block of cheese. Every few months this was delivered to our reserve in Saanich, where we lived for a time.

My dad did some manual work delivering coal to homes around Victoria. It was heavy labour and dirty work. He came home every day covered in coal dust. He was overworked but it supported our family. He was always in a good mood, and I think he was proud that he was able to bring home some income for his family.

When I was four or five years old, I would accompany him to cut wood on our land in Saanich. He would use the long, crosscut saw that was around five feet long to knock down trees and cut wood for us. He was a very kind, softhearted man, with a corny sense of humor. He always thought of others around him.

He taught me respect at a young age, especially for Elders or those less fortunate. Such a wonderful considerate man with great basic principles to share with me. A lot of his words still remain with me today.

My late grandfather Francis James was born December 1874. He passed in fall of 1973. My youngest sister Becky is seated on his right and my wife Lorraine seated on the sofa arm.

My late mom's dad, my grandpa Francis, came to visit his daughters at the residential school one day with my grandmother Matilda and their youngest child Rella. He had his boat anchored below the residential school, and it was very early in the morning before daybreak when he arrived. He and my grandmother were going to visit their two daughters, my mom Lavina and her sister Ramona, after early morning mass.

He got dressed and went above the deck of the boat, while my grandmother was below dressing their daughter Rella. She could not find one of Rella's shoes and she leaned over too far and bumped the gas or kerosene lamp over. It immediately set a fire below the deck. My grandfather ran down into the flames grabbing my grandmother and my young aunt Rella, who was about two years old. Rella died immediately from burn injuries. My grandmother was taken to the infirmary at the school. She was there for three days but died from burns also.

My grandfather's hair and his clothing were totally burnt but he was very strong and brave for trying to rescue his family. He healed to live on for decades longer. Thankfully, this helped me as I spent so much time with him and learned a lot from him as he shared a great deal of traditional knowledge when he talked of the old days in his life.

He was always so quiet and kind with everyone. His second wife Josephine died before him. He later came to live with my aunt Mary, his oldest daughter. He had a bedroom adjacent to mine. Some early mornings, around two or three a.m., I would awaken and walk by his room and see him rubbing his legs. I would go and get his liniment and rub his legs for him as they were cramping. He would soon get relief and I would sit with him and he would just talk with me, sharing old stories and ways with me in his soft gentle voice. This was quite a regular event for us, and I adored his gentle demeanor. He had a quiet, soft laugh. He smiled and his whole face smiled, and his eyes, too.

This fire tragedy must have been very difficult for my late mom and her sister Ramona, to have this happen while they lived at the Kuper Island Residential School. It was also a difficult time for my grandfather to lose part of his family on this sad day. My late aunt Mary shared this with me. She, like my late mom Lavina, was so petite in stature and very loving and caring to us. She always called me son when we talked together. Her voice was always soft and gentle when she spoke to anyone and her eyes and face showed her gentle ways.

My mother Lavina passed away in the state of Washington. Our two aunts Ramona (my mother's younger sister) and Mary (her oldest sister), took us into their homes and cared for us, treating us as their own children. They were two very special women to me, as my aunty Ramona had her own family already, and my aunty Mary was well into her retirement years.

They both filled in the mother parts for me that I sorely missed as a teenager. They both stood by me, being my conscience, always offering support and love to me during my youthful years. Especially when I was disobedient and getting into mischief, they were both patient with me during those trying times. I may have been scolded for my actions, but it was always within good reason to show me boundaries and good judgment.

Mary fostered my brothers and myself, beginning the fall of 1963, on Kuper Island. Her husband, my uncle Simon, was a very quiet man and so gentle. I never heard him raise his voice at all. He was such a proud man that he wouldn't ask anyone for help. He always just did things himself, so honorable.

He rarely spoke but was one of those guys with smiley warm eyes when he was around people. "Hi my cousin," he would often say. This was his greeting to all the other men his age, when he saw them. Another one of his phrases was "Oh my gosh, cousin." This was his regular greeting to all the men he saw because he was happy to see them. When he smiled, his whole face was smiley, and his thick eyebrows were so prominent, too. He was a lean man, around six feet tall, and always wore his fedora hat when he was outside.

I sure miss him and my aunty both, as they were great people to be around every day. They both left me with warm loving impressions that guide me today as I emulate them and their ways of tenderness. This keeps me connected to them both.

Aunty Mary would knit sweaters from raw sheep wool, soaking it, washing it and drying it. Then she would tease the wool, put it through her grinder making it into bales of wool and then spin it into yarn. After that she would make it into rolls with each u and then place them into her knitting basket alongside her wooden needles. I would assist her sometimes with teasing. It was very tedious work going through this knitting, but it was her contribution to the family's monthly income.

Uncle Simon was a night watchman for the Kuper Residential School. We lived in a one-room house that was about 20 feet x 16 feet. This always impressed me, the way of our people. If a parent passed away in your life, family members would immediately step in to support and assist. This is what my aunt and uncle did. It was a demanding job to take on for them, with no financial help from anyone. They both filled in the parental role so easily and unselfishly.

I love them both for doing this today and have so much respect for them as well, for providing a loving home environment for us. Day in and day out they parented us without a single complaint.

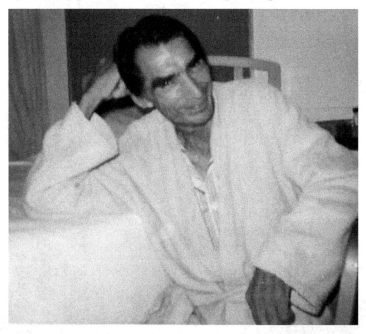

My late uncle Simon was a compassionate, kind, loving soul with a big heart. A very proud man who never asked anyone for help and liked to do things for himself. A very tireless man who worked all night at the Kuper Island Residential School as a night watchman and sat at the table most mornings with his usual black coffee and smoking a cigarette. Then he would go lay down and sleep during the day, to rest for his work for the upcoming night.

Uncle Simon had a woodshed next to the house where he stored a harness for Sue, an old family horse that he used to get firewood for the house. He used a wood sled to load the wood and transport it down to the village, while walking next to the sled. He harvested wood for heating the house, never asking for help. Once in a while I would help chop wood. There weren't any vehicles on the island yet, so Sue was the only means to help harvest the wood.

Sue would wander the island so he had to bring a rope and go out and get her so he could go up to the woods to cut a tree for firewood to heat the house over the winter.

My late aunt Mary, here with my son Adrian. She was such a kind, tender loving woman with a big heart. She is well into her seventies here.

My sweet late aunty Ramona (left) and aunt Mary (right) handily filled in the role of mother support to me, in my young years. I miss them both for the love and patience they showed me. Sometimes they could have been tough on me but they remained steadfast in their loving ways with their treatment of me.

CHAPTER 7

I Meet Lorraine and We Start Our Family

In 1972 I graduated from Carson Graham High School, in North Vancouver. I was offered a job in Alberta with the Department of Indian Affairs. I refused it but took a summer job in Vancouver working for the Vancouver Indian Friendship Centre, working with children who lived around Vancouver, mainly around the Hastings and Main area. This job required setting up activities, programs, tours and crafts as a summer day program for them.

Every day I was up very early, before regular work hours. I would get on the early bus with rolls of dimes used for bus fare for children at each bus stop. This was because the children were very young so I felt I needed to be there for them.

I worked with four other youth that were chosen to operate this program, including Lorraine, a northern girl from Alert Bay on Cormorant Island. This summer job was with young children mostly under 12 years of age who needed activities for the summer. We set up arts and crafts, swimming lessons, and tours around Vancouver. We even went to the aquarium and zoo among other areas of interest to the children.

There was also a week stay at a camp towards the end of the summer. I was able to help with beading bracelets and more and one of my close friends, Bob, helped with looms.

This young girl, Lorraine, was smitten with me. One weekend she went out and bought the same clothing outfit as mine and came to work with it on. It made me feel awkward to see her clothing exactly like mine. She was always hanging around me during work breaks, chatting and smiling at me. It was so clear she wanted more from me, a relationship that I never ventured in before.

Lorraine and I drew up the whole summer program for the children. She did some macramé teaching with the young ones. One needs a lot of energy for a job like this but we had some beautiful times with the young children.

It was a socially awkward situation for me to be in with someone infatuated with me, but I started to finally become close to a female. My guards were now coming down. We began long chats during lunches and breaks getting to know each other.

We did our work for a couple of weeks together, so I asked her out to watch a soccer game. The great Brazilian soccer player Pelé was coming to Vancouver to play soccer with the New York Cosmos team. I bought tickets for my brothers who lived on Kuper Island but they were unable to make it, so I asked Lorraine to come with me.

She came to the game and loved it, screaming, cheering and jumping up and down. Full of energy she was. Happily, we started to date, going to the beaches in Vancouver, swimming, movies, many trips to Stanley Park for picnics, sharing good times, and getting to know each other.

I took Lorraine out for a pizza one evening and later on she told me that it was her first time to have a pizza. This was a surprise for me. Although she barely ate one piece, we just seemed to hit it off together. My first real relationship was starting with a young girl who was so determined to build a relationship with me. Initially it was so awkward for me but I gave it little thought and continued to see her.

Lorraine and myself with her dad Christopher on Granville Street in Vancouver taken by a professional street photographer in 1972.

Thankfully it worked for us, as up to that period of my life I had many doubts of my self-worth and didn't know if I could have a functioning relationship with anyone at this point. After the sex abuse from those Catholic brothers, I had many doubts around myself and figured I could not offer much to anyone at all, especially a young girl, as I had a lot of hang-ups that I didn't deal with as a young man.

Lorraine was able to dispel these feelings in me, by her openness and willingness to spend time with me. Her energy was accepting and open with me and all my guards were coming down. It warmed my heart. I learned how to have fun, to be uninhibited and carefree once again.

I was supposed to go to Langara College in Vancouver at the end of summer but Lorraine felt I should try college in Victoria, as she would be completing her high school there. I applied there so we could be together. I also began to board with her grandparents, Chief Tom Hunt and his wife Emma. It was a neat experience for me to live in their home with them as a young student.

That whole year was a treat to be with them both. They always spoke their own language to each other. I was given their traditional foods for my meals. Some mornings I would wake up to Tommy playing music with his accordion, or squeeze box as we called it, all by himself sitting on his chair in the living room. During this time his wife Emma was helping with the set-up of displays at the provincial museum in Victoria. I enjoyed my time with them both, but I failed my college big time.

It was quite a challenge to have five social sciences courses to take, along with the large textbooks for reading and study. Much of it was beyond me at the time, as I was undisciplined and on my own.

I began to look for work around Victoria but there was nothing available for me. I returned home to my aunty and uncle's place. My uncle Simon was not well so I filled in at job as a night watchman for five months at the Kuper Island Residential School.

Lorraine graduated from Victoria High School in 1973 and moved in with me. She worked at the residential school with young girls there. We rented a home in Chemainus after I got a job at the sawmill. I had been a pain to them, phoning them morning and night every day, so they finally gave me shifts for work. I just made it into the union, but was out of work again as they went on strike.

Meanwhile, Lorraine was expecting a child. Tony Jr. was born in January 1974, which was a huge change for us both. Shortly after his birth we moved to Penelakut Island (formerly called Kuper Island) where I began to work with my tribe in the area of social work and education. Later on, I did only the social services position. I now had steady income, but sadly I spent many weekends going to cabarets, having a lot of alcohol and thinking I was having fun. Today I know it was simply an avenue to forget all the residential school abuse experiences I had and was holding inside of me. It wasn't good as it was unbalancing my life.

One day I returned home with my wife Lorraine from our night at the cabaret with friends and we went to the babysitter's place to pick up little Tony. I was exhausted and had had very little sleep. I carried my son into our tiny living room. He was still in his diaper as he was fifteen or sixteen months old. He made that hand motion which he learned, pointing to his mouth, asking for food because he was hungry. I went into the kitchen and picked up a box of Ritz crackers and gave him a couple, which he ate eagerly.

Feeling tired, I had to lay down on our sofa and I fell asleep. I woke up a couple of hours later. Glancing down I could see my son sleeping on the floor in his diaper. It was touching to see this tiny soul lying there. All alone and helpless, this little innocent child. It grasped my heart strings.

I decided to get up to move him on the sofa and cover him with a blanket. As I began to sit up, I was shocked to see a pile of Ritz crackers piled where I was sleeping, below my chest. My son took a bite out of each cracker and placed them by me in a pile. I almost cried. I felt so guilty as my son had needed me and I went to sleep on him. It was a heart tugging experience for me. I decided I needed to be a dad and devote my time to being a good dad. This now became my priority. Alcohol and my regular outings took a backseat.

We were blessed with another son, Adrian, born in 1978. He was a big boy weighing over 11 pounds. Shortly after he was born, we went through marriage problems that continued for well over a year. Adrian was a little over two years old when we made amends and my wife and I then figured on another child. Kyle was born in 1982, which solidified our marriage. I continued my job with my tribe which kept me busy doing social services for 37 years until my retirement in 2009.

I became very busy with my three sons as they played hockey, baseball, soccer, basketball, lacrosse, rugby and so on. Practices and games meant we had to leave the island a lot. I was proud of my sons. I loved that they were able to play sports in the community with other young boys.

But there were some prejudiced parents that made it hard on my sons sometimes, because hardly any First Nations children had the opportunity to play sports in public.

My three sons Kyle, Adrian and Tony Jr. who kept us busy in all the sports they played. I am so proud of them for their efforts as youth. They even coached some teams as they got older.

A couple of my sons played on rep teams with the better players. I made it my priority to keep them all in team sports, to provide healthy relations for them and experience good times with friends in the outer community. We taxied a lot of their teammates who were from single parent homes. My wife and I gave thousands of hours to our sons and their sports, but we were happy to invest time with them.

One morning, around 1986, wife Lorraine said, "We have to go shopping," I replied, "Go ahead but take the boys with you."

They all got dressed up and headed for the ferry. Lorraine said, "I will call you later," I nodded to her, "OK". As soon as they left, I went down to the basement, searching for something.

Walking around down there I soon found what I had been looking for. I grabbed it and carried it back upstairs to the living room and sat down. I was in a daze. I sat there in deep thought.

Losing track of time, I finally began to unroll it and spread it out. I then took one end to make a noose out of it. This rope was 30 feet long. I finished making the noose and sat there wondering where I should go with the rope.

My chaotic mindset was so deep into taking my life. I really felt I had no worth or purpose any longer. I was standing in the deep end feeling lost and helpless. There was absolutely nothing for me now. I was hurting and feeling dirty. The abuses that occurred to me were in my face and I had no one to talk to at all about these feelings. I couldn't ignore them and just wanted them to end.

I felt I had no choice, as I couldn't contain my thoughts or feelings any longer. They were burdensome for me and difficult to have on my mind day in and day out. I assure you that thinking about this was not on purpose.

Today I feel that perhaps this is one of the hardest things for a person, suffering in isolation. This is not purposeful but ends up that way. This seemed the easiest way to finish my internal battle. I was going to put an end to the pains and misery of my troubled mind.

Just then the phone began to ring and ring. I sat there ignoring it but finally I pushed myself up because it kept ringing. I walked over from my chair, reaching over to grab it and said, "Hello." It was Lorraine. She just said, "What's wrong? Your voice sounds funny!" I tried to talk but my stumbling words were not coming out right. My wife said again, "What's wrong?" There was lots of desperation in her voice, "Talk to me," she said.

My voice was animated. It didn't sound like me at all. Lorraine kept me on the phone just talking to me for over 20 minutes. She finally began to connect with me. My voice was beginning to sound normal again, and a bit more comforting. "We will be on the next ferry," she said. She had no idea what was on my mind that day. If I hadn't picked up the phone, I wouldn't be here today.

Many survivors go through incidents like the one I just shared but they succeed in ending their painful and miserable days. It is very difficult having thoughts of ending your life because some days are unbearable, remembering what happened to you, sexual and physical abuse. Or even losing great friends or family members, these overbearing feelings manifest themselves deep within us. We lose hope and sense of direction with our life. It was like a huge upheaval of heaviness. I am very thankful that I didn't follow through on my actions and thoughts.

I actually shared this event with a men's group at a conference, as I know many young ones have no idea what challenges their parents or grandparents had at residential schools. This sharing was a glimpse into the impacts we deal with in our lives. Sadly, many actually end their lives in agony and in isolation.

Ironically, isolation and silence seem to be our protection. But what from? With our reality, our pains, our memories and our struggles we isolate ourselves for too long because of shame. This shame doesn't belong to us. It has to go to the abusers for taking advantage of youth and helpless children.

These abusers should be reported to the law as it may help other adults who suffered at the hands of these abusers. Many victims probably thought they were the only ones abused, as that's what I thought myself. Those who were abused are large in numbers as I learned later. Many were dealing with the same feelings that I had all my life.

Today it is my honest feeling that whether the abusers are dead or alive they should be reported to the police. I sincerely urge our survivors to step forward. But get some help or support first, from a friend, a family member or even support from a professional if it is available.

This is vital as it may help other survivors who were abused. Believe this survivor. It was very rough on me, giving my statement to the RCMP before the criminal cases began. Do it, as it may help you find peace someday.

CHAPTER 8

A Painful Disclosure to My Wife

One of the most challenging days I ever faced in my life began as I was going to bed one night in 1987 when I was 36 years old. I had a routine every night as I got to my side of the bed. I would reach for a little night light that I stored in my bed table. I would always plug it in before going to sleep.

I then began pulling the blanket over myself. I lay on my side of the bed and closed my eyes. Lorraine softly says to me, "Why do you need the night light on?" I said, "I don't want to stub my toe in the dark." But "why?" she says again, so I simply said, "I don't want to bang my knee on the bed." But "why?" she says again. Getting very frustrated with her I answer again. Once more she said "why". I can't believe we are going through this at bedtime. I answered her about ten times. By this time my voice was climbing with each answer.

But she persisted. "But why?" I finally blurted out to her, "I was sexually abused in the dark!"

Up to this point I had never said a word to anyone nor had a discussion about sex abuse. I hesitantly disclosed to my wife. Breaking down, I then began to cry. My body shook uncontrollably. She grabbed me and squeezed me tightly. I lay in her arms crying for over three hours like a baby. I then told her about the sex abuse from the two Catholic brothers.

My long-buried secret finally came out from the depths, making me vulnerable and fragile. I could no longer hide it from her or myself. As this painful release came out, the loving support of my wife helped me face this huge hurdle, where I had been stuck for decades. Her simple question opened the door to a painful past.

My outfall of tears was an avenue, to rid some of the huge pain I carried. I really didn't know it at the time, but my disclosure was a relief. It was a chance to tear down the walls I built around the sex and physical abuses. I feel that it was a protection that I needed for myself until such a time as I could talk about it freely. Now at least someone knew, my wife and trusted confidant. We never talked about this again, but my tears were telltale enough, I suppose, as it opened the agonizing door for me.

Disclosure of sexual abuse means the door is wide open. I felt it was important to get some counselling for myself. I had a visit to the family doctor where we had a lengthy discussion about my abuse. When we ended our discussion he said, "I will look and check into finding someone you can see for help." It seemed to end right there. The doctor never got back to me for counselling. Apparently, there was nothing out there at all for survivors, at least not specific for residential school issues, which are all so intertwined with one another, making it complex.

CHAPTER 9

Kuper Island on Film:
My Brother's Abuse

Not too long after the appointment with my doctor, in the late 1980s, I met up with my cousin Diane H. She informed me there was a film being made about Kuper Island Residential School and asked me if I would be interested in getting involved with the project. I agreed that I would, so she said that she would talk to the film crew to express my interest.

I soon connected with Christine Welsh, a respected documentary film producer and director, on the phone. She said that she would like to interview my brother James and myself on film. After giving me all the information, I agreed to be filmed. A date was settled upon that the crew would be coming to Kuper Island to film my brother James and myself together.

Up to this point, I had done an interview on film for public television in Germany and an interview with a German student for her thesis about residential school survivors. I also was interviewed by another group during which I talked about art and my life. They were from Germany too.

The film crew arrived and we headed down to the Penelakut Spit, down at the point on a beautiful sunny day. For filming with my brother and myself, we just found a shady spot on a log, above the beach, sitting together. This was just above the shoreline. Christine took a seat in front of us to the side. Being with my younger brother made it easier for me doing the interview. We had some general discussion that we would stay away from some heavy material for this film.

My brother James and myself had just found out through discussion, that we were both sexually abused. Up to this time in my life I had no clue that my brother had the same painful experiences as myself at the residential school. It was disturbing and heartbreaking for the both of us, but we were troupers during the filming and did the interview.

Today this film is being used in many of the universities across Canada to educate students about residential schools. It is available on YouTube.

The film is called *Kuper Island, Return to the Healing Circle*. We also went for a stroll together down the beach as we were wired with microphones for this part in the film.

The premiere was held at a theatre in Victoria. After it was played, my brother James, late Delmar and myself were asked to come onto the stage. All the people in the audience lined up and gave us hugs. There were over three hundred of our people there who came for the film. Many of them were crying and hugging us tightly, giving thanks for the film about residential school.

They were so thankful to us for making this film as it was ground-breaking in a way, as there were not too many films about residential schools at the time. It was completed in 1997. Sadly, many of the survivors who were in this film have passed on to the spirit world. But my brother James and I are still here, for which I am so grateful for today.

I became very close to late Bill Seward as he was in the film. We became friends as we went through the Independent Assessment Process together. (The IAP provided support for group members, families and communities as part of the reconciliation process) I sure miss his sensitive, kind nature as he was older and always shared what was on his mind. Such an honorable man, I will never forget him. Bill was so knowledgeable and connected to the history of our people. He could talk about it so easily and it came out well, just like it did in the film. We spent a lot of time together, some days reminiscing about events from the residential school at Kuper Island.

My connection with him, in many ways, has helped me today when I speak in public because he was so honest in all the words he shared.

CHAPTER 10

Our Court Case Against
Our Sex Abuser Begins

In the late 1990s stories began coming out about residential schools in British Columbia. Many survivors were beginning to speak about their sexual abuse and physical abuse mainly from the Port Alberni students who were very vocal about what occurred with "Plint", a sex abuser.

I was contacted by some of the students from Kuper Island. They were feeling that we should do something about what happened to us at Kuper Island Residential School. I was told we would meet with a lawyer from Vancouver who was working on his own. He was willing to represent survivors, at Kuper Island, to start legal action for our abuses.

We began by having many meetings with this lawyer, each talking with him about our abuses. We were getting together every three or four months and were asked to refresh our minds about what abuse we had, and from who, and when. We had to be very clear, as not all abuses would be covered in this lawsuit.

We were also meeting with Crown counsel to discuss legal proceedings against Glen Doughty, the man who had abused so many of us. This began in 2001 when we had a meeting with Crown counsel, Stan Lowe from Victoria, as there would be a criminal investigation into sex abuse by Glen Doughty. There were thirteen of us from Kuper Island involved, young men who gave statements to Crown counsel individually. We all felt that Doughty should be charged criminally for abusing us. We were never allowed to speak to each other about abuses from Doughty.

I personally felt there should have been some kind of consequence for what he did to me. I shared with Crown counsel my experience with Brother Doughty, who was my supervisor at Kuper Island Residential School.

We met with Crown counsel a couple of times. He said a date and site for our case would happen in Nanaimo. We all agreed that it would be the best place to have our case heard although we had an option for

Vancouver or Victoria. We would individually be cross-examined in court about our encounters of sexual abuse from Doughty.

I remember Lowe stating to us, "You will be able to watch Doughty get cuffed and led away in court. This could be your closure."

In the fall of 2002, all 13 of us were brought to a hotel in Nanaimo for the week. Rooms were booked for us but we were still not allowed to speak to one another. Crown counsel approached me and said, "You are our main witness. You will be on the stand longer than the rest of the guys."

We were just finishing our meeting with Crown counsel when I met up with Charlene Belleau who was assisting the Residential School Commission. She came to Nanaimo to support and witness our court proceedings. I sat with her for about an hour, first thanking her then talking with her about my case. She was very supportive and listened carefully. Meanwhile, I noticed a priest sitting across from us in his black clergy outfit.

He walked over to me and knelt down beside me and began to cry. He then said, "I am sorry!" He kept talking apologetically. I just said, "Excuse me I don't know you." He replied, "I came up from Victoria for our hearing. I am sorry." I just told him, "You have nothing to be sorry about, you didn't do anything to me!" Being a bit perturbed I ignored him and continued my discussion with Belleau. We just smiled to each other then she wished me good luck.

The other men did their appearances in court to testify against Doughty. I finally received a phone call at my room. It was Crown counsel Stan Lowe who gave me a time to be at court to give my testimony. I was so tired of being in the hotel room by myself, just watching TV and eating my meals there. I would be the last witness who would be testifying against Doughty.

The next morning, I got to the court building by myself and was met by a number of people who greeted me. They were from our Shaker Church. They took me to a small room and prayed for me. After their services I was given a candle. They burned that for me and it was to support and offer me prayers to bring me strength. I was very thankful to them as I was alone for my session in court.

It meant so much to have support from these people who wanted to be there and help us. Moral support was so valuable at this time, especially since I would be talking about sex abuse that Doughty put me through as a teenager.

I sat outside the courtroom, feeling very apprehensive about being there. A court deputy finally came and called my name. I came forward and she said, "Please follow me." So I did, walking from behind into the courtroom. She pointed me to a seat below the judge. A deputy came over to me with a Bible and I took an oath to tell the truth. Then I was seated on the chair facing the people in court. I looked around and was shocked to see Doughty sitting directly before me. He was about eight feet in front of me sitting at one of two tables. I went through formalities stating my name, where I was from, and information about Kuper Island Residential School, and such.

To this day, it was shocking for me to put my hands on the Bible of all things! And to testify against my abuser who was from the Catholic Church. It was conflicting for me to be put in this aggravating situation.

Then the laborious questioning began. I sat there all day on the stand answering questions about Doughty and incidents we had together. I am sure every question I answered was given to me again and again with the change of only one word. I was truthful and honest to them for every answer but it was tough on me as Doughty sat there looking at me the whole day.

At one point the judge asked me, "Can you tell us what you have in your hand?" I simply said that it was a prayer candle given to me by the Shaker Church faith who are offering prayers for me today. I was beginning to get exhausted from my ordeal sitting up on the stand, being grilled with tons of questions from Doughty's church lawyers. The judge finally said, "We will end our court session today. I will require Raymond to be here again tomorrow morning."

For the two whole days I only looked at Doughty once as I sat on the stand giving testimony against him. I was facing everyone in the courtroom and if I looked at them directly it would have broken me down.

I looked above their heads, as I didn't want to lose my train of thought because I wanted to fully answer their questions. I was so nervous and wanted off the stand and to leave. I was so uncomfortable knowing that he was in front of me, after decades of trying to erase him and my memories of him.

The next morning I sat outside the courtroom, again by myself, waiting for my court appearance to begin. No one was sitting around me at all and my head was slightly down as I sat on my chair. Through the side of my eyes I could see a black figure. I looked up and noticed this person in a black raincoat. It was Doughty. He noticed that I could see him. He then backed away from my gaze, not looking behind. He just kept walking out of my sight never even looking back at all.

Soon the court was in session again and I sat on the stand going through very much the same type of questioning as the day before. I never relented in my quiet, slow answering manner to the lawyer. After the two hours or so of questioning we broke for lunch. Then I had to return to complete their examination of me. I did two days on the stand and I recall there being some legal discussion and the judge saying he would pronounce his verdict the next day and I would now be able to return to my hotel room. I was exhausted.

The next day, the thirteen of us who were involved in the case against Glen Doughty gathered and entered the courtroom. We all were seated in an area that is normally used for the jury. Doughty came into the court and was seated in a section for those on trial. It was boxed off and surrounded by plexiglass. He sat there by himself with his head down.

Justice James Shabbits came into court and discussed the case. He looked at Doughty and asked him if he had anything to say. Doughty stood up and looked at the judge, not looking at the thirteen of us at all, who he sexually abused. He just said that he was regretful for what he did and was sorry for his actions.

Justice Shabbits sentenced Doughty to three years in prison. He then exited the courtroom.

All thirteen of us sat there waiting for Doughty to be handcuffed by the sheriff. But the sheriff said, "Now I ask you all to exit the courtroom." The people in the gallery of the courtroom then left. We were all still standing there in the jury duty area when the sheriff came over and said, "Please leave now." One of the guys said, "We were told we could watch Doughty be cuffed and led out of the courtroom!" The sheriff said, "Leave!" All of our group stood up and left the courtroom.

Our closure never occurred as we were forced out of the courtroom.

Incredible. He only got three years in prison for messing up our lives, for sexually abusing us, even after he did the same things at Williams Lake Residential School earlier in his career. I feel this was a small sentence for his sex abuse to us. We were affected by his abuse for the rest of our lives, every single minute. He should have received a longer prison sentence. I have very little faith in Canada's court system for cases around residential school abuses.

Up to this point, there were no individual counseling services available to survivors of the abuses to us, especially the sexual abuse, that occurred to us usually at a very young age. Many of the young men had a hard time talking of it. It was a struggle for many of them. There was no counselor to sit with us at all. Our support was nil during this trying time in court. No one had a clue of the sex abuse we had been through, nor did they know of the challenges we had in court with Doughty and the legal process.

It took many years before treatment or counseling services were available to survivors at all. Especially counseling that specific. We lost a great range of things that included loss of our language and culture. We had family breakdowns and loss of connections to our community. It was not only physical, sexual or mental abuse but also so much of it was piled one upon the other, making it a complex issue to speak of. That is what I feel, as a survivor.

My counselor, Frank, asked me to write up my issues weekly in the best manner I could so we could work on it at my pace for healing. This, of course, was very tough working through tears, anger, resentment and reluctance in some areas. However, this process allowed me to write memories and painful times I lived with for years.

My counselor patiently moved me to a healing point with myself. I no longer broke down crying as I spoke to him. I was very thankful for his patience, which allowed me to become a stable person today with full acceptance of myself now. I have a greater degree of peace in my mind and in my heart. There is no more guilt or the blame I carried for so long in my life towards myself.

Counseling, for me, was learning and understanding the individual issues I had and the many problems I faced as a survivor. It allowed me to finally sleep and rest fully at night, with no more restlessness. It helped me immensely to understand that I was the victim of abuses: physical, mental and sexual.

My counselor told me, basically, that we come to a standstill from the point of abuse. Especially when it happened to us at a young age. We have to allow the younger me to learn that I was abused and was a victim. This is very complex to write, I just hope it sounds right.

Most of my life I carried the burden of blame and guilt, which hindered me as a person, as I struggled to get past the events in my mind. The younger me had to heal and allow the young boy to move past those painful events of abuse.

The biggest part for me was learning to forgive my abuser, which I felt would not be possible for me to do. But in reality, we come to a point in our healing when we must let everything go, because if we don't, it will continue to be a part of our life, causing havoc, pain and more. But this release enables me to live more peacefully now.

I feel that the blame is the biggest area we deal with as victims. We seem to take this on to ourselves, even though we were very young when we had abuse. I learned I am not to take any blame, guilt or responsibility for what happened to me. This must go to the abuser. Since we had no choice or options as youth available to us at the time.

The court system provided no closure and little in the way of justice for myself and the other children who were victims of Glen Doughty at Kuper Island Residential School.

CHAPTER 11

Painful Settlement Process for Residential School Survivors

Our lawyer, who looked after compensation for residential school abuses, said we were one of the first groups in Canada to be compensated for abuse. The process would be an IAP – Independent Assessment Process, where a lawyer for the government, my lawyer, and one from the Catholic Church, would decide my settlement.

When I had my hearing at the large hotel boardroom, I walked into the room with almost 30 people. Lawyers from the church bishop's office, the federal government and more were present. I had to introduce myself to them. I said that I didn't want to continue until I knew who was at the table with me. There were so many of them. They each got up to tell me their names and titles. It was a bit intimidating just to begin this process with them as I had no clue why they had such a large number of people here to settle with me.

I sat at this meeting with three large binders, which were searches for education, work and health. There was a lot of information about me, my siblings, my parents, and my foster parents that were written in these binders. They represented a profile compilation of me that included a lot of the history that they required. This information was all directly from me. I spent a large amount of time writing all the information. I had to sit there as they queried me about the information in the binders.

During the meeting, each of them would challenge me in one area, and say things like, "Your education was not so good so you probably would not amount to much in your life!" And, "Your parents were alcoholics, so they probably were not very good parents to you." And this one, "You are in poor health right now; you don't take very good care of yourself." I sat there listening to them, as they each had negative things to say to me, from these three binders. They only found negative things to comment about regarding myself, or my parents. It was upsetting for me, and so hurtful to listen to.

At one point I talked about how well my sons are doing now, in school and all their activities but they never responded to me at all. This whole process was making me feel low and not very good about myself. These people were heartless and ruthless in what they said to me. My energy was being drained totally. They finally decided it was time for a break and to leave the room together. They would go over their notes and discuss my case for a monetary settlement while I waited in another room.

My lawyer looked at me as he came back from talking with them in the other room. "This is what they would like to give you for your settlement. What do you think?" I said, "That sure is low!" He would leave the room and go speak with them again. They upped the amount a bit but not much. My lawyer says, "This is a pretty good offer, maybe you should take it. If you leave it you may not get anything for your settlement." I relented and gave in to their last offer but was not happy with it because we had waited over five years to get to this point.

He then told me what would be taken from my settlement: his legal fees, court costs and the costs for searches on education, health and employment.

It all seemed so grim. The comments from the committee of almost 30 people; includes things like "your alcoholic parents," "your poor education," "you will not amount to very much." Not one kind word to me at all. I just wanted out of this whole situation and to be done with it. We spent three or four hours listening to them knock me down, any way they could. I was very belittled by this process. It took me days to compile the information required, for all the areas they needed. I was only criticized for failure. I was too honest, I suppose. It was basically used against me in every area of my life.

The same kind of questioning came from them all, each of them concentrated in one area to deal with me. I certainly wish I had the same amount of people to query them for what happened to me at the residential school. For days later I didn't feel good about myself any longer. Their low settlement offer to me was nothing but an exercise of shaming, with humiliation and indignation. It may not have been their goal, but it left me with those feelings.

The small award I received didn't soothe me at all as it still left the hurts of all the abuses I suffered. Was it to compensate me? I really built myself up for this process but it only acknowledged that I was sexually abused. I probably was looking to feel better about myself for what happened to me but I just never could get to that feeling. I still had the same feeling and challenges and I suffered from obesity which brought many complications for my health.

When costs were deducted it was less than half the amount awarded to me. The lawyer deducted more money from us as he said that some got low amounts so they could not pay him much. Those who received more would pay a bit more from their settlements.

We had to meet with our lawyer to receive our settlements. When we were awarded, he wrote out cheques from his personal account. We were upset because we had hoped they would be bank drafts so we could cash them right away. Instead, we had to wait a few days before the cheque cleared the bank. We felt it was a tacky move by the lawyer as he always reminded us that he was using his own money on us.

There was so much turmoil from this process. I was aggravated with it all. My lawyer said, "You can take your binders with you now!" I looked at him and said, "I don't want them, you can keep them!" They all had so much of my history of my life, including that of both my late parents which I disclosed to the committee. It made me feel uneasy and unsettled within myself, but I spoke mostly from anger for what they said to me and the way they said it.

Today I feel that there is absolutely no conscience shown by the Canadian government for their treatment of residential school survivors. Especially the questionable handling of our cases during settlements, with some delayed or dropped entirely for vulnerable survivors.

Just to be involved with these actions for any survivor is intense, stressful and heart tugging for many of them. This is mainly because of poor records by churches or the administrators who didn't keep proper records or entered wrong information on student files. This, no doubt, was assisted by Canada as some of our claims were minimized.

When many survivors were required to make a statement or give information about their abuse, they may have been in a traumatic state, like myself, which didn't help them or me at all as we were still hurting and had so much pain. This affected the outcome and it caused the process not to work in our favor and resulted in very small settlements for us. During this time we also didn't have any support systems in place. I feel this made it unfair and worked in favor of Canada and the churches.

A few years ago, the federal government awarded a Syrian man over $10 million for treatment he received in prison. How is this so when residential school survivors spent ten or twelve years of their lives in a residential school being sexually abused and physically abused, losing their family, language and culture? Some received paltry sums of $2,000 from Canada. I personally fail to see this as a justifiable settlement to survivors for the painful times they had at residential schools. I know, as I struggled personally for a long time, that survivors across these lands must have had the same difficulties.

I am sure there must have been some kind of support given to the Syrian man, with assistance to him, to talk about his settlement and such. There was absolutely nothing for our survivors to support them or assist them, while they spoke about their experiences at residential schools.

Last year I sat, as an Elder, with a claimant at his hearing. He did well in his settlement. I contacted his lawyer directly and he came to see me personally. I informed him that I settled and was upset for what happened to me. He said, "If you settled today you would start at (a much larger figure)." I received less than a quarter of this amount. Later, he got back to me and said that I signed the agreement at my settlement hearing which said I would no longer pursue my case. So, I had no options available.

He said, "Maybe you should contact your lawyer that you used for your settlement." So I called him. His answer was, "Maybe you could sue me. There is nothing else you can do." All the current claims today don't have the deductions we had, I believe, from the settlements they were given.

A claimant, who actually settled after me, thanked me for my initial moves to the settlement process and criminal court for residential school, as it helped survivors later.

This IAP process was very flawed from the start, as the process changed as did as the settlements. The resolution of early cases had absolutely no merit except for being an indicator for upcoming settlements in the future.

My group was part of the earlier settlements given which were very low with more than half our settlements going to legal costs, job search, education search and such. All those who settled later did not have to be financially responsible for these deductions from their settlements. I realize money is not the answer for us, but it remains a sore point for me as I was offered so little for my abuses, and I reluctantly accepted. I used it for bills. I had hoped to go for a trip somewhere but couldn't.

CHAPTER 12

Health Issues

In 2003, early one morning, I was up for my coffee, showered and dressed. It was 7 a.m., time to head for my ferry from Chemainus to work on Penelakut Island. I walked outside this early March morning and got into my wife's vehicle, started it up and left.

I approached the old wooden bridge not far down the road from where I live. It had a slight curve as you approach it. In an instant the vehicle began to slide, then it rammed into the bridge and I became airborne. The rear of the van was up in the air, then I went forward, hitting the steering wheel with my stomach area. I looked down at it and noticed it was bent. The van was now sliding backwards towards the other end of the bridge. I was groggy and just sat there as it finally came to a stop. A couple of people came up to the van and told me to keep still as I may be injured. Within a few minutes I could hear a siren from the direction I came from. It was an RCMP officer. He stopped at the entrance of the bridge, got out of his vehicle, closed the door, and started to walk towards me. He immediately slipped and fell as the whole bridge was caked with ice. He made it to the van and asked me if I was OK. I nodded yes.

He said an ambulance had been called for me. Within minutes, Chemainus or Crofton firemen arrived with ambulance attendants. It took them 20 minutes to remove me and put me onto a stretcher. I was transported to the hospital in Duncan, examined, then released by the doctor and given medicine.

The red area on my stomach became infected with cellulitis and began to swell. This was hard and very difficult as I was almost 300 pounds. This infection stayed with me for over five years. I eventually weighed over 350 pounds. My physician said, "Hopefully you will last, if this medicine stops working you will die!"

It is important here to share just a bit of information about my weight. I feel it began to be become a problem for me when I had triggers or flashbacks about my residential school abuse and trauma. It seemed I was trying to comfort myself with food. As I did this, I was not very active either. Weight issues started for me as I became a larger man. It was during this time there was absolutely no one for me to talk about the sexual and physical abuses I suffered at the two residential schools. The abuses had started to become an emotional problem for me.

Our own tribal doctor was an older, almost retired English doctor. He said, "Tony, if you need to see a doctor go to Victoria emergency as they have all the specialists there to help you."

I spent many weekends there with my wife Lorraine at emergency. One day when I was very sick, my wife called her sister Deb who suggested I go to see Dr. Spence, her doctor. So we did, at Victoria Jubilee Hospital. He said, "If you came in later today or tomorrow you would have been dead." I was in very poor health. I was immediately hospitalized and given treatment at the Royal Jubilee Hospital.

Meanwhile, I was seeing a gastric bypass doctor for over three years who said, "You have to lose some weight so we can move ahead with surgery." I had a scheduled date for surgery and was brought in for that particular day by my wife Lorraine. She told him that I had some sores beneath my stomach area but apparently he didn't hear my wife.

I went into pre-op and a specialist came over to see me. "We will be putting you under gas for your surgery," he said. That's all I can remember. I came to later and the gastric bypass doctor said, "We had to cancel your surgery. I noticed you have some lesions on your lower abdomen area. You may get an infection. Luckily, we cancelled your surgery. You were under gas for 10 minutes. If you went through the full surgery procedure you would not have made it. The sleeping gas mixture was not good. It took over two hours to bring you out of the sleep, even though it was only 10 minutes of sleeping gas."

Thankfully my gastric bypass doctor was able to find a skilled young surgeon, Dr. Taylor, who would do the surgery to remove the cellulitis-infected area from my lower abdomen. Many doctors were asked but they all refused. This kind doctor had to make an incision from one hip to the other, to remove the infected areas. It was over 60 pounds from my abdomen that he removed and he had to rejoin me by using over 160 steel staples.

I had to leave the hospital and stay in a local motel for a week. Finally, I went to the hospital but none of the nurses wanted to take the staples out. It was the surgeon who eventually did. Later I went to a florist and bought the most beautiful bouquet of flowers available and dropped them off at his office. I was very grateful he was willing to do the surgery when no other doctor would. He gave me a new lease on life and a keener sense of it.

I used to sit on my La-Z-Boy watching TV. One day my granddaughter, who was five years old, came over to me. Christina noticed something. I had no shirt on so she says, "You have no belly button!" I said, "Babe the doctor had to remove it because I was very sick. I didn't need it." She felt very sad for me.

She then says to me, "I will draw one for you. OK?" She got a pen and drew one for me on my stomach. It melted my heart. "I love it. Thank you babe," I said to her. Then I gave her a big hug for her thoughtful gesture. Children can be so insightful.

Children can be so understanding no matter what their age. My granddaughter was so thoughtful and caring at this age, noticing I had no belly button and wanting to help me. Her beautiful gesture meant so much to me, especially because she was such a young child.

My granddaughter Christina who loved me and encouraged me to get well. She drew a belly button on me because I didn't have one anymore after my operation.

When our health is poor, we are so susceptible to more challenges in our overall physical condition. My gastric-bypass operation was scheduled and finally completed by the doctor when I was healthy enough for it. He then went for his holidays. Before he left, he said there would be a doctor to take his place, as I was still in the hospital. She soon released me as a patient so I went home, but within a short period of time I was getting very sick. The fill-in doctor, for my gastric bypass doctor, should have prescribed medicine for me, as we are prone to ulcers from this type of operation.

I couldn't hold down any food or liquids at all. Nothing was staying in my stomach, so Lorraine brought me back to the hospital in Victoria. I was immediately admitted and my doctor gave me a familiar message. "If you came in tomorrow it would have been too late, you would have died." Another close call. I eventually would have a hospital stay of six months. My stomach was covered with ulcers, which prevented me from eating or drinking fluids. My stomach actually turned around inside as I became very sick and weak.

I was so weak since, a little over four months earlier, I was over 300 pounds and obese and now I was a bit over 100 pounds. I couldn't even lift my head if I needed to drink or eat. The nurses who were a daily support for me had to spoon-feed me (usually soup or Jello) for my daily food to rebuild me.

These caring nurses would kindly say, "Open your mouth Mr. Charlie, you need to eat." They kept encouraging me every day to eat because I didn't want to anymore. I lost my willpower and motivation for food. I would just look at it but had no desire to eat any of it. I have such a great respect for the nurses now. They had to do this for me every day for my meals before I had any strength to feed myself.

Slowly I was gaining strength and would sit up on my hospital bed. Frequently, I was pushed around by wheelchair. I was so tired of my bed, just lying there on it every day. But I was so grateful for my late aunt Georgiana, my late dad's cousin, who always came to visit me. She had to catch three different buses to get to the hospital. "Hi nephew," I would hear. I would turn and look to see my aunty smiling at me. She was always so cheerful and had a beautiful smiley face for me. She was always very encouraging to me when she spoke. She was always positive too. I loved her energy and her attitude.

She inspired me with her simple encouraging words of hope, reminding me of family and good days ahead. She always called me "son" every time she saw me. I just loved her and I am so thankful for her today as she cared for me as only family can, and loved me, inspiring me by the attitude she displayed.

My other frequent visitor was my sister Janice who bused from her home up-Island, to come and visit me. We would share coffee and goodies or she would get me magazines to read. These two were so supportive through their regular visits with me. During this time their contact was important for me since I felt alone in the hospital environment, being hospitalized for such a long period of time.

My wife was always there for me, despite challenges, as our funds were depleting now. She would come when she could. Even the hospital parking was expensive and would add up, using up our meager funds very quickly.

After four months I began to see a physiotherapist. The first thing she said was, "You will have to learn how to stand, walk and balance yourself again. Your leg muscles have gotten so weak now." When we began my physio, I had to stand between two parallel bars and learn how to balance on one foot. Then I had to learn how to take steps, one by one with goals of five steps and graduating to ten steps. After weeks of effort, I began to walk on my own. I had to wheelchair myself to the physio room to have my workout and then return to my bed.

I was sometimes taken to the TV room next to the hospice area and I would be left there. I sat on a comfy sofa by myself in back of the room. I would just sit there many days, not even watching TV. During these quiet, trying times I began to examine myself, my life, my condition and my situation.

I decided that I had a lot to be grateful for: my family, my job, my sons and my wife. This helped me and made me more determined to get well and find energy to walk, even though it was tiring taking those small steps.

I felt very deeply that I needed to be there with them. As I did this, I began to feel good and peaceful for myself. My mindset was changing now, I wanted to live and share my life with my family. Previously I didn't care for anything, my willpower was basically gone.

On two separate occasions as I sat on the sofa in the back of the room, I was approached by individuals who quietly asked me, "Excuse me sir, are you a holy man or a spiritual man?" I simply looked up and smiled to them and said, "No, I am healing myself and trying to get strong." My simple approach was learning to love and respect myself, love my beautiful family, and make myself well.

I had decided to change my mindset, find my inner peace and my strength because I wanted to be well in both my mind and my body!

This was key for me because previously I never liked myself at all. I honestly felt I could not offer anything to myself, or anyone, with my background of being abused at the residential school.

One of my doctors, an older fella, used to come to my room. He would say, "What are you doing lying there in bed?" I just said, "I just came in from my walk." He would say, "Get up and go for another one!" He was almost demanding to me, the bold aggressive way he would say, "Just walk across the hall, then walk 50 steps. Now walk to the end of the hallway." He was always setting goals for me and sometimes I despised him for treating me the way he did. He was very abrupt with me and so direct. Those small walks were very exhausting for me to do and I was so tired after each walk.

In reality, he was helping me to become strong again by forcing me to walk, by motivating me with his unique, demanding style of encouragement. It seemed harsh and crude to me but now I see that he was asking me to challenge myself to set my own goals and walk. Pretty soon I was doubling my exercise routine every day in physio on my own because I was so tired of the hospital. And the food, too.

The day finally came for me to be released as a patient, after my stay of six months.

Before I left Victoria, I asked my wife to go to a chocolate store called Purdy's. I bought some fancy chocolates and dropped off three boxes with a thank you note at the nurse's station. I felt so grateful for their support, kindness and assistance at the Royal Jubilee Hospital.

I finally came home but I could not climb the stairs at all. My son Kyle and his friend carried me upstairs. My heart was so warm being in the comfort of my own home and my familiar surroundings and being able to sit back in my own chair.

The reality was that I was not very strong yet. I had to get a bus to Duncan for physio for a few weeks and buy some weights for exercising my arms. I needed large elastic bands to use daily, to help strengthen my legs by attaching them to the dining table legs and doing leg lifts. I had to rely on my walker and cane full-time around my home.

My wife Lorraine was still working at the time. One day I fell down on the living room floor. I desperately tried to get up but could not. I was stuck on the floor almost four hours until my wife returned home. She immediately helped me up off the floor. It took almost six months until my legs were strong enough that I could be steady on my feet again.

My daily meals for months were still mushroom soup or oysters. I couldn't eat anything else at all. No other foods would stay down in my stomach.

My weak, unsteady legs required me to use a cane. My health had further challenges as I had gotten gangrene internally which took my gall bladder and part of my liver.

While my health was declining, my wife herself was actually in the hospital from where she had just phoned me. We talked on the telephone for a few minutes and she hung up. But she had forgotten something that she wanted to mention to me so she called back right away. I had hung the phone back on the receiver less than three feet from where I sat, but when it began to ring, I could not reach it. I tried really hard, but I began to get very dizzy and disoriented. I was getting very frantic and feeling very helpless. I had no idea what was happening and began to barf up blood.

I was beginning to have a massive hemorrhage! Blood was exiting from every opening in my body. My son was sleeping at the end of the hall. I tried to call to him for help but I had hardly any strength or voice.

My wife then called her sister who kept phoning and finally spoke to my son who called the ambulance and it came immediately. I was on it for almost an hour as they attempted to insert an intravenous line into my arm. They gave up as my veins were collapsed. They began their treatment by giving me five pints of blood. Surgery and medication were given for my ailment, during my six-week stay in hospital, until my energy returned, and I was released to go home.

I am now 71 years old. I don't need my cane or walker any longer but I do periodically still lose my balance or get unsteady on my feet. This is mainly because of arthritis in my left knee. I still want to strengthen it by not using my cane. I was forced to retire from my managerial job of 37 years because of my health. I gave up the use of my cane over six years ago. I should still use it but I refuse. I walk but it is usually not very fast. I still get to where I am going but it is a feat for me some days.

CHAPTER 13

Speaking My Truth

One day when I was with my Elder group/Cultural Connections to do a workshop at Langara College in Vancouver, I went with Elder Ron to the First Nations area of the facility. Outside one of the offices was a huge drum in the seating section. Ron beat it for a while, he is a traditional singer and carries his drum with him.

Just then a young lady came out to us so we chatted with her. She said she was getting ready to watch a movie with a class so I asked what the movie was. She mentioned the title, Kuper Island, Return to the Healing Circle. So, I just said that I was in it. "Oh my God," she said and rushed over and hugged me. "Thank you!" It is hard to believe our movie is still being watched 25 years later, but it is good as it brings a message of informing and educating, though painful, for those who watch it.

The whole issue was just starting to surface across Canada at the time we filmed this movie in the late 1980s. I believe I could have been more descriptive in it but we felt, at the time, it should not be heavy. We had so many survivors who were in a tender state during the filming of the movie. It is so evident when one watches it.

I am very fortunate that periodically I get requests to speak at agencies or organizations to share my story as a survivor. I am now confident and have absolutely no problem speaking. One of my very early supporters was my son Adrian. He always said, "Dad you should go out and speak, as you are good at it."

Today I can speak about colonialism, my residential school experiences, or our own local history from our tribe. I sincerely feel much of this is important to remember and share as not much is known by the general public today, especially about residential schools and its impact on our First Nations people across Canada.

One day a dear close friend, Dr. Kelly Bannister, asked me to talk to a group at the University of Victoria's Centre for Global Studies. They were all professors, staff and PhD students, numbering around 30 from around the world. Initially I felt intimidated to do so but I felt they were here to listen to me. I spoke about reconciliation from my viewpoint. I was honest with them and spoke of our historical treatment we received from colonial governments and churches. This was only the second time speaking solo to a group but it was a start for me. It seems so far back now but it was an experience for me.

I also speak locally at the schools to young children when invited. I speak about art, as I am an artist who draws and carves masks, bowls, spoons, rattles, totems and more. I share information about our culture and our lives as a people, on the light side, enough for them to understand us. Along with this I share our history, which I share about colonialism and what occurred to our people.

My good friend Dr. Kelly Bannister invited me to speak to a group at the University of Victoria. This was a relatively new experience for me but it bolstered my confidence and I now enjoy the many speaking opportunities that come my way.

This is an emotional part for me, as we were forbidden to speak our language, practise our culture and gather with our people. Here is an experience I had as a child. At our tribal school in Brentwood Bay, one morning during recess, around six of us children sat in a circle. We were singing songs from our longhouse when all of a sudden a Catholic nun stepped into the middle of our group. She started yelling, "Stop! What you are doing is evil! That is why their faces are painted and they have pointed sticks! They are devils!" She stood in the middle of our little circle, looking down at each of us, screaming this to us.

This was a traumatic experience for me that occurred at such a young age, it remains so vivid for me yet today. It has affected me my whole life. I still have a mental block because of this sad occurrence. I try to sing today, with our men when they drum and sing to our groups. I force myself to sing. As when we sing, it's a natural experience for us. Today I continue to try and sing but with difficulty.

One of my first speaking events was at Our Place Society, which assists homeless people in Victoria who live on the streets. I was asked by my Facebook friend Fred Roland to do a talk, two sessions all day for the staff and volunteers who work there. There were around 300 people but the two groups had 40 to 50 in each that I spoke to. I shared my story as a survivor, which was painful and honest. I had had no counseling or healing at this time. However, I did connect with the staff and the impacts I disclosed were touching to them. I ended my talk with a thank you to them all for working with the homeless people.

For many of them, it was a reminder of colonial occurrences in their countries, including treatment, pain, loss and horrific memories. They came and shook my hand or hugged me. I found my voice that day, which has helped me immensely. I carry no doubts about my abilities for speaking to groups.

I have been very conscious of my words to the young children when I speak, as their ages are quite varied. Young elementary school children only need to hear very basic information, but when I speak to older children I can be more open with them about my experiences. As some schools hear about me, I get requests to speak as I have been to five local schools to speak to children about residential schools. I basically share general information as I don't want to be heavy to them about certain hardships.

During my many talks I have had Jewish people, Africans and Australians come speak to me with stories of similar treatment from around the world. Many of them hugged me and thanked me for sharing. I was so thankful for the invite by my son Adrian Charlie who works at the BC Ferry head office to give a talk with staff there.

I have, along with my brother James, decided to become involved in another film, *Kuper Island Return to the Healing Circle, Part 2*. It will be released in 2002, though a lot of people from the first film have passed away.

I speak at schools sharing my culture, art and some stories about residential schools. Here I am speaking to a Grade 7 class. I am so grateful that my cousin Laura Antoine took this picture as I spoke to the class of elementary school children at Crofton. She has been a supporter who knows my story and the journey I have been through as a survivor.

I continue to get invitations to speak to children at schools. I will always make time for them as it's an important opportunity to connect with them.

CHAPTER 14

Working with Men's Groups

I have been fortunate during my retirement. As my pension benefits had not yet begun for me, I was asked by our health society to work with three different men's groups with the tribes involved with the agency. I then began to teach basic carving with two young groups and cooking/baking with men from my tribe.

This was an opportunity that I was very thankful for mainly to the health agency that served four different communities including my tribe. In total, there were between thirty and fifty young men of various ages. I found this work to be challenging but rewarding to watch them build interests in carving, cooking and baking. Yes, men are great at cooking and I often shared that on Facebook. We got tons of neat comments and even a request came in to do a cookbook!

It is evident that men in our communities are frequently left out in programs in most places. Almost all agency areas have programming for women, pre-natal women, or moms. These are important but men should also be included, as we need to build healthy men and dads too. I was fortunate to work with these groups for four years until funding became a problem with these vital programs. Men enjoy being together, which is great as it gets them away from home, builds relationships and provides for a healthy learning situation for them. Many of them gained personal confidence for themselves and generally felt better working alongside other men.

One day, I had an intense headache, so uncomfortable for me, so I went to the nurse's office. As our program was at the Health Centre, the nurse felt we should check my blood pressure. Surprisingly it was high and in the danger zone so she recommended that I see my doctor, which I did. He immediately started me on medication for this condition of high blood pressure.

I was very lucky to have a nurse, Michelle, close by to assist me so I spoke to her about men's health as we had some diabetic men involved.

Michelle, Men's group and I then began to have weekly sessions and discussions around high blood pressure, strokes, diabetes, aneurisms and more. Our men were able to get excellent information from our nurse, Michelle, about their health. I felt this was a great program we started with the men of my tribe.

As the information they gained from our nurse was helpful to their lives and health as men, I shared information about our activities on Facebook and we had many followers during our sessions. They were excited to see the young carvers and loved to see the foods we made or the baking done by the men.

I try to stay busy and focus on being well. I had one and a half years of counseling for residential school issues and it helped me immensely. My counselor, Frank, encouraged me to write this book.

I have a voice now that I feel I must use to share my story. I will continue to do whatever possible in hopes of bringing awareness for those survivors who have no voice today by giving insights into our struggles and complex issues we live with today.

I have had all the same pain and challenges so I can speak directly of my experiences. I honour you all beautiful resilient survivors today, for being here on Mother Earth. Our days may be numbered but we survive!

When I speak, I have found it is no longer an issue to share my feelings, thoughts or experiences. I feel I must connect with the audience so they understand what I am sharing. Sometimes it has been tiresome and challenging for me as it can drain oneself when speaking of trauma. Usually, my mind prepares what I am going to say a day ahead. Some days it is exhausting and very tiresome and I feel drained physically after my talks.

I rehearse in my mind what I am going to share, with hopes to make valid points that can be supported and felt by those who I speak to during my time with them.

Later on, after my talks, I have found that eventually my mind and body are able to recover and I find later I sleep peacefully. I no longer have a need for a nightlight or lights. The room is dark and it is no longer a problem for me.

I no longer break down when I speak, shed tears or show anger. I know that tears do show I am vulnerable as a person but I am now past that part. Tears make me forget the words that I want to say so I try to maintain composure when I speak. Periodically I do feel anger, but don't want to be known for anger or remembered for being angry.

Much of my anger still goes to the churches and our Canadian governments where it should be directed to, for what they did to our peoples in the residential schools they operated across Canada for 120 years, devastating our children and families.

I feel I cannot be complacent, because I am a grandfather now and it is a role I relish wholeheartedly. These things must never happen again to our people, we cannot afford to take a back seat any longer to any abuse. Nor should our people be subjected to abuse from anyone. I am hopeful that by sharing, it will help improve situations through awareness. We need protection for our young ones today, so they can stay healthy and strong and be proud, unhindered by anything in their paths.

They need to recognize that they have gifts from their ancestors that are being restored, such as our beautiful art, history, language and traditional ways of the past, which were forbidden at one time for our people. I sincerely hope they will remain proud of their heritage, as they have no limits for themselves.

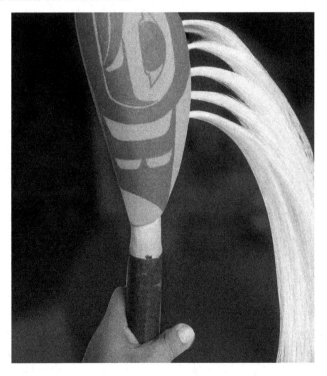

Here is a salmon rattle that I made, designed and painted myself. Made from maple wood, hollowed and inserted steel beads for sound. I used horsetail hair for the top of the rattle.

Especially in terms of education, jobs, and talents, I feel we are all blessed with gifts individually. My passion has always been art. I love to draw and carve in wood. I have been carving for over 40 years, making rattles, totems, frontlets, masks, paddles and more. It has brought me immense contentment and peace many times when I struggled. This is a part of my inner strength that maintains me in a peaceful position. At my best, I would carve for fourteen to sixteen hours at one time, immersing myself into art. No doubt it helped to stabilize my life, which helped ground me as a person. I have been so thankful for my ability to carve.

It makes me happy and proud to see daily gains by our young ones in our communities. They are doing great but we need more of them to take professional roles as doctors, lawyers, teachers and such to help our people. Their potential is by far more promising than that of residential school survivors who have personal issues to deal with. Some survivors do very well, but on the whole I think most survivors who were abused still have struggles and issues.

It is my hope that our youth remember themselves and their people, when they achieve their degrees. It is vital that they support and show the young ones anything is possible. I ask you to show or support someone so they can follow in your footsteps as I feel every person can achieve their dreams with effort and determination, but they may need support behind them.

My next hope is that through my prayers, our survivors will seek help and heal. It is important that we move away from harsh treatment we experienced and lived with as survivors of residential schools. Don't give up hope as you are still here. Find your healing for yourself as a survivor. I just can't believe my healing has brought me tremendous change in my direction, my ways and confidence.

I personally feel Canada and the churches have to continue to support us to become healthy again today, as they are jointly responsible for family breakdowns, loss of language, culture and pride.

The Catholic Church and other churches have spawned abusers in our communities today to further complicate our healing journey. It continues to impact our families greatly. When our people report sex abusers from the church it is important that the church acts responsibly to our people.

I feel that the church should bring these abusers forward immediately so that the abusers can face legal charges in the courts. It is very important as victims need closure and positive actions for sex abuse that occurred to them from church priests, nuns and brothers at residential schools. Countless times today, when a victim steps forward to report sexual abuse, they have to wait for action from the church. This is not acceptable because the abusers go into hiding and the law has to do a search.

To Canada and the government today, I want you to remember that you are still responsible for the actions of starting residential schools. It is a very difficult time for residential school survivors, as many of them do not have access to support in their communities today and this is a huge concern. Survivors should not have to suffer and carry burdens of their memories from abusive times at residential schools. It not only affects them, but the whole family and community who must still deal with hardships, as survivors sometimes become abusers.

These residential schools have affected many generations including great grandparents, grandparents, parents, brothers and sisters today. I have met many of them who carry so much pain and trauma because of abuses they had at residential schools. Their difficulties remain a real challenge for many of them, as they don't know who to speak to regarding the abuse they had from their caregivers that included priests, brothers, nuns and other staff at residential schools.

We are in need of supportive programs and staff to assist us to heal. They should be long-term programs that we can connect with to help us have healing. The bouts of sexual and physical abuse that they recall is very traumatic for many of the survivors who turn to alcohol or drugs.

Language is important and vital to our First Nations peoples' culture. My Hul'qumi'num language is in danger. It is only spoken fluently by one per cent of our people today. Our language must be protected! The Government of Canada along with churches are directly responsible for this dire situation today. They are accountable for their actions.

We must also remember that there are intergenerational children who have seen or experienced the abuse directly by their parents or grandparents who have displayed some of it in their lives, unfortunately. We should not have to live with these horrendous pains today, as we were victims. We must assist these young ones especially, so they can learn about trauma and be healthy. They are very precious to our communities.

We must move from these abusive times as people. I point to the Catholic Church because they operated the residential schools I attended as a youth. Other churches, as well, basically brought the same damages and hurtful experiences to our children across Canada.

Today, I have no fears of speaking about my experiences as a survivor of residential schools. I always feel I need to be grounded as a person with an open mind. I need to be someone who will not judge others. They should be respected, as I have no clue of their lives. But they will learn mine so that they can have an insight into the lives of our people. The residential school survivors and their families still experience trauma and pains.

I have personally found that speaking of my abuses and the trauma I experienced at residential schools has helped me to heal because it is an admittance of a huge issue I carried that has impacted me for such a long period of time.

There continues to be so much to be said as a survivor, but it is difficult and complicated right now. We have mounds of issues to live and deal with, such as low self-esteem, broken families, struggles of poor health in addition to drug and alcohol abuse.

We need support and understanding to deal with these issues and problems we have from residential schools. It is vital for a promise to a better time and days ahead in our future as healthy First Nations people.

CHAPTER 15

Speaking to the Truth and Reconciliation Commission

In 2012, there was talk about the Truth and Reconciliation Commission having events across Canada. I discovered there would be one here in the Cowichan Valley. The Truth and Reconciliation Commission of Canada (TRC) was created through a legal settlement between residential school survivors, the Assembly of First Nations, Inuit representatives and the parties responsible for creation and operation of the schools; the federal government and the churches. The TRC travelled the country hearing personal experiences from survivors, communities and families personally affected by the residential school experience.

I was very emotional when I gave my testimony before the Truth and Reconciliation Commission in Duncan a few years ago. I was 61 at the time and spoke of abuse I suffered five decades earlier.

It would be in Duncan at what was once the Heritage Centre. I called the person who was coordinating the event and she told me to prepare my statement. I spent about four days writing my statement on my computer. I wanted to cover my events as a survivor.

I arrived at the event early, checking in at the registry area where I met up with the coordinator. I asked her when it would be my turn to speak. She called me aside and said, "Can you open the conference?" I was surprised by her offer, but I agreed. So, I walked to the front of the room to find a seat.

I could see two elevated tables in front of me. The Chief of the tribe walked in and took a seat next to me. We shook hands and briefly spoke to each other. A few minutes later my nephew, Chuck, walked up and said, "Hi uncle." We chatted briefly, then soon the Chief and my nephew got together and went to the front, on the side of the room, and talked with each other. The room started to get more crowded as people were coming in and sitting. This event was open to the public and it was getting loud behind me with all the chatter.

A group of drummers walked in with a couple of Elders and gathered at the front. The Chief welcomed the survivors and everyone with special thanks to the Elders for being present. A prayer was given in our Hul'qumi'num language and a song was given for thanks and strength to the survivors.

My nephew then outlined the process for the TRC, as he would be the chairperson. He, in fact, was the "Siem" that would be coordinating each day. He informed survivors that they have two options available, they could give their statement publicly or give it privately at the back of the room where private rooms were set up for them. The public one would be before the commissioner.

Chuck then introduced the commissioner, Ms. Marie Wilson, who would take the statement on behalf of the TRC. She was already seated at her table. As I would begin, my Hul'qumi'num name was called, then my English name Raymond T. Charlie. Grabbing my cane, I walked up to the elevated table. As I sat down, nephew Rocky came over and asked if he could support me. I agreed, so he sat down next to me. With my nephew Chuck on my right, I pulled out my papers and put them on the table. I respectfully thanked the commissioner for taking my statement.

I began to read my statement. I slowly lost track of time as this was getting emotional for me. It was my direct admission that I was sexually abused and now my wounds were showing. I couldn't hold back my feelings any longer and I broke into tears momentarily and tried to compose myself. There was an Elder listening to me on my left in front of the room and he was crying as he listened to me. I finally finished my statement and walked off the stage area and was looking for a place to sit.

A co-worker that I worked with for years came to me and gave me a hug. She said, "Sorry that happened to you." I walked a few more feet and my cousin Cherie came up and gave me a tight hug. I neared my seating area to the side of the room and my friend Charlie said, "You almost talked for an hour!" I wondered why my nephew was tapping me on my shoulder. I was only supposed to speak for 20 minutes! I felt it was challenging to give a statement when we were still having traumatic times yet as survivors. As we talk about our hard times at the residential schools, that is painful for us.

Many of us were in tender and sensitive states as survivors. Time restraints may be difficult to adhere to when talking and sharing our horrific times we had. I know there must be time limits in place and it probably was a hard thing to start out this way as I used more than my set time.

Today I lift my hands and give heartfelt thanks to those brave survivors who shared publicly. It certainly was very difficult and hard for you. Canada and the public needed to hear from us all, the dark secrets of abuse to us at residential schools. So very unfortunate, though, as many survivors still have trauma issues and struggle daily.

This TRC process has shown directly the evidence of the horrid treatment we received at residential schools from 1876 to 1996. I have shared so much directly on my Facebook page and many shared back to me, through Messenger or my posts. It was so disheartening to hear the abuses they endured from priests, nuns, or brothers.

Their experiences which they shared with me personally were horrid. Many are from my local community here on Vancouver Island. I have so much respect for my beautiful friends but I cannot share their stories.

Today we have abusers in our communities who attended residential schools, who abuse family or people physically and sexually. They were hurt, so now they begin to abuse people in our communities. This is so sad. It is shocking and hurtful to see and hear we have to contend with this amongst our people. It breaks my heart.

But I want to inform and educate the public of our abuses we have to live with as a result of going to residential schools. It's our grim reality we have to live with and deal with every day of our lives. It still continues to affect so many of us in different ways with hardships. We need support and understanding so we can get the necessary help with these issues.

There are horrendous events throughout our history at our residential school, which were talked about when I started there. A vivid discussion I remember was the story of newborn babies being tossed into the huge steel incinerator on the grounds at the far end of the soccer field. This was below the gym at Kuper Island. Or the bodies being buried beneath the apple tree or thrown into the ocean. I did share earlier that graves were found on the far side, opposite the residential school.

So many youth never returned home to their families. So many starved or got sick and died.

There were always stories of the young ones trying to leave the Island. As I mentioned earlier, a couple of young boys even tried to use a log to get to Chemainus but drowned. This happened while my cousin Richard was still there. So sad to hear of young children trying to leave the residential school. We lost thousands of children who died at residential schools across Canada. The actual number may never be known but at the time of writing it has been determined that more than 7,000 graves have been found. I doubt we will ever know the number because of questionable records that were kept at the time and the reluctance of the church to share the documentation that they may have. I suspect much of it has been destroyed.

CHAPTER 16

The School is Gone:
The Memories Remain

Some time ago our tribe received funding to take down the Kuper Island Residential School, so a company brought in two large excavators. When almost every window was broken it reminded me of the scars in the lives of our people. For decades people from other areas had a difficult time walking past this building when they came to our reserve for cultural events or funerals. This was because of the harsh times their family has suffered here, so much trauma and memories for them. Many people would just put their head down or turn their gaze away from this building.

I was just returning from lunch at my home when I could see the two large excavators had begun to work. Each machine was taking swathes of it, floor by floor, so I rushed home for my camera. I took tons of pictures of the work in progress. It was so weird as I was the only witness there. Perhaps it was the best way as it was not a loss at all to our people. Today I can take out the pictures I took of the work bringing the building down. I have not shown them to many people because it may trigger negative emotions for some survivors.

In its place an adult school, daycare and health centre were built, but some concrete stairs still remain. Hopefully they will be removed.

This huge red brick building was on Kuper Island and had an intake of children from the 19 Vancouver Island tribes, starting with Qualicum south to Victoria and surrounding tribes. It was built on my reserve of Penelakut, initially down on the seashore, placed on the western side of Kuper Island. Below this building was a long wharf that had moored boats for the school. The first building was a wooden structure built in 1890 and replaced after about 20 years after a fire destroyed the original structure. It was built up on the hill facing Chemainus on Vancouver Island.

This four-storey red brick building with two wings was completed in 1912. It would replace the old wooden structure that was down on the seashore. This new one started out as an industrial school, where most of the children at this time worked the fields on the farm behind the residential school. The girls usually did the sewing and such while living there and my late uncle Simon did various tasks when he attended this school.

Uncle Simon told me he did farm chores, worked in the kitchen and was even forced to kill the pigs and cows with a sledgehammer, out at the barn. During this time, he had only 15 minutes of schooling per day. Every day he had to work the farmed area for food that would be grown for the residential school. Some of the young boys had to chop wood for the boilers that heated the building. The wood was harvested directly from Penelakut Island.

Strangely, it looked new when I was there in the mid-sixties. It was bright red and it was so clean and seemed out of place in the southern Gulf Islands, as you may only see this type of building in the city. It was so out of place, but, of course, that was done on purpose.

I know in my heart that as survivors our lives may seem normal but that is far from the truth. We do regular things every day: work, family activities and more but it's only a routine that pulls us through each day. I know, as that's what got me through for many years. It's that old thought: if we ignore our problems it will be fine. That may be so but these problems, though dormant, fester inside us silently, manifesting themselves in many areas: our minds, our health and our well-being, breaking us down.

I know a few survivors who are older than myself. I share with them my story and learn theirs too. Some are exactly like me, carrying so much pain and trauma but they have found peace for themselves. I feel that the main support is from understanding and loving spouses, which helps a great deal. It is so precious to have understanding and supportive spouses. We are so grateful for them and the support they give.

We are in dire need of healing and restoration of basics in our lives today, to make us strong in our families, our beliefs, our culture and language. As many of us struggle with much of this today, I feel personally it is the residential school trauma and experiences. I lost our beautiful language because my late mother chose not to teach us because her generation was punished for speaking it at the residential school.

Today I will point my finger directly to the Government of Canada for this huge loss, as well as the Catholic Church who stood idly by doing nothing to assist survivors, but they had enforced the harsh policy of

Canada. The richest church in the world has made no efforts to assist healing for survivors for all the sex and physical abuses they inflicted on children at residential schools they operated.

I understand the Catholic Church operated 60 per cent of the residential schools in Canada. Money is not the solution, but they should help put in place programs that will help rebuild our people to independence and a place of self-reliance for survivors and their families. This is so important to reconnect with our cultural ways, language or even building self-esteem! Today it's not always possible as we continue to lose leaders, cultural teachers, and Elders. They hold so much history of our traditions, language and culture. This is all key to our people and our pride.

Some areas have lost so much as culture, language and traditions were denied at residential schools because Canada did not allow us to use them and harshly punished children for doing so, especially around urban areas.

The Kuper Island Residential School was built directly on my tribe's reserve. Two of them – one was destroyed by fire – were constructed and used for over a century. We bore the shame, even though we had no say in constructing this building on our land. The government just built them without our consent.

There is, of course, so much more in terms of the genocide, as spoken now by Sen. Murray Sinclair. This includes the medical experiments that were carried out at these residential schools. Mr. Sinclair did a tremendous job with the Truth and Reconciliation Commission. I have huge respect for him and his voice, bringing awareness and findings to Canada and the world.

My late uncle spoke about the injections that were given to children. He said the hardest part was that the doctors and medical practitioners who injected the children, just stood there as the children staggered and fell from the effects of being poked. Our children were used as guinea pigs for experiments carried out at residential schools. The doctors were hoping to learn more about the effects of malnutrition and other health issues.

These experiments were horrendous in the 1940s as over 1,000 children were deliberately starved at residential schools across the country. This was an insane act against our innocent children that we must never forget, as it was cruel and unthinkable. I was told that in Germany, Hitler used some of the same procedures that had been used in Canada's residential schools.

These colonial acts by the governments and churches using residential schools are long lasting with negative impacts. It is my sincere feeling that we have become an industry for Canada, and that is clearly seen by the sheer number of agencies, organizations and people who continue to work caring for our people today: social workers, prison guards, foster homes and such, some providing questionable services. These numbers must be staggering as they work with our people daily Are they really helping or are we just fodder for their industries?

Our people struggle and fail in so many areas. Many programs fail our people as they are designed for the population at large, which is hugely different from First Nations people's direct needs. It is slowly changing but barely improving. We continue to have large numbers of our people, including children, in prisons, foster care and jails.

Today I hear of many of our communities with sex abusers. As they were sexually abused, they become abusers themselves. It is a sad legacy of residential schools, which continues to hurt our people across the lands.

Since we are not healed, we come into conflict in various areas every day, sadly, with all the laws and regulations set up by colonial governments with no input from our people. We continue with these ways today, consistently being on the wrong end with these agencies.

Dealing with unfair laws, history and mindsets, we will always be on the wrong end. My feeling is that much of this can change if one has residential school impacts noted in their background. The impacts must be considered, much like the Gladue reports for our people that are present in the court system.

The Gladue reports are a compilation of an individual's history which may include residential school history of themselves or family members. If they come before the court, it helps to show how their history has impacted their lives. Not all courts in Canada use Gladue reports, which are made by specially trained writers who research families and events (including residential school survivor history) or connections with others in the community.

I assure you we don't look for pity, but it helps to understand us and what occurred to us at residential schools across Canada. It's still the darkest secret in our history.

This must and should be a part of reconciliation as we have to overcome this sad part of our lives. We shall see, as it has felt like Canada wants to bury all our statements that we gave during the Truth and Reconciliation events that were held across Canada. They would like to destroy our records but we can't let this happen. There was so much heartache and genuine information shared about our abuses at residential schools. I feel they must be maintained for our youth and our future as it's a look into our history and the horrific treatment we received by Canada.

Though painful for our people, we must remember residential schools and know the facts as they affected many of our people across Canada. We need to preserve all statements given by survivors. Some may be confidential but available to families of the individual. This, of course, is much like the crimes against the Jewish people. Atrocities, neglect and forcing our children into residential schools is our experience and we can't let anyone off the hook in this important matter.

We must always remember how residential schools were part of a sad time in our history and we cannot let that knowledge slip away. It consumed too many lives of our people, our culture, traditions and language. Canada is using its colonial laws and court system to erase our stories and experiences. I feel our records must be saved for our future generations, as they need to know and remember the stories and experiences of their family members who went to residential school.

Today, some of our people do not speak their language, practise their culture, or have the information about their families or where they are from. Their families are broken. This is a direct result of the actions of Canada, a country that banned our culture, our language and started residential schools for our First Nations people. It was all in the name of assimilation and what was nothing short of genocide. This drastically affected our people, as residential schools existed for 120 years. It still impacts us today with many of the issues I mentioned earlier. I feel this has proven to be a thorn in our lives because churches who operated residential schools followed directions enforcing the regulations set out by Canadian governments.

I sat with my Elders of our Tribe and we were given a presentation by the University of British Columbia, about children's gravesites. They used scanner equipment over the residential school ground on Penelakut Island and discovered 26 burial plots that were unmarked or recorded. There will be more areas of the grounds scanned on the residential school site. These were children borne by young girls who attended the Kuper Island Residential School. Much more work needs to be done.

It is important for us as a tribe and many families who lost children at this residential school to seek answers. Our residential school at Kuper Island had many missing children. Sadly, we are in the top five of all the residential schools in terms of children not being returned to their families for one reason or another.

One night I went to the theatre with my wife Lorraine, to watch the movie *Indian Horse.* It was hard for me as many of the events in the movie were like mine. I made it to the end of the movie but was taken aback by the seemingly nice priest. What he had done to the nice young boy was like my sex abuse from Doughty. I choked back some tears at the difficult part for a few seconds and had to compose myself. I was glad the theatre was dark as no one knew, not even my wife, that I fought back tears. I wiped my eyes dry, as this was a huge trigger for me and I had to keep my mind strong.

I applaud the late writer Richard Wagamese, along with Clint Eastwood, for making this movie. I feel that the depiction and appearances of the priest was right on. Nice? No way, but it shows clearly how we trust and then are hurt by these phony people that are cloaked as people of their god.

It will take awhile before the non-Indians catch on to our residential school horrors, but this movie will help them to grasp it. Of course, it touched upon many of my direct experiences but not all the horrors of our residential schools, such as murders of young babies and children, or the medical experiments that were done.

This photo was taken in Vancouver at a BC Ferry and Marine Workers Union Convention of over 150 members. Many were moved by what I shared with them. It's always interesting to meet with many people of First Nations ancestry who come to speak with me later. Their families had some harsh times too, at the residential schools.

CHAPTER 17

Reflections

One of my concerns as a dad is very basic when I think of my three sons. Did I do a good job as a dad? Have I been supportive enough? Have I been a good example to them? All I could really do some days was love them, as parenting can be delicate and challenging today.

I had no intentions of holding them back from their goals. They, like anyone, have great potential as men, and are capable of most things in this life. I want them to dream, travel and see this bigger world. When I worked, I was able to save and take them to California to Disneyland, Las Vegas, and Kona, Hawaii for some special times with them. But, of course, all I want is for them to be proud of themselves for what they do every day and be happy in their lives.

Today it is my goal to be healthy in mind and body. I won't be held back any longer by the abusive times that I had at residential schools.

I love to do simple things like having coffee daily with wife Lorraine, going to the movies with her and enjoying activities with the grandchildren when I can. I adore my beautiful grandchildren Christina, Jesse, Brooke and Kyle. I also remember my granddaughter in the USA, Rachel (Charlie) King, who I think about and love dearly, too. We regret we are not part of your life today but we think of you constantly and love you Rachel. You are a member of this family along with the other grandchildren.

I am very hopeful for the future of our people, with thoughts of all our grandchildren and young people out there who can forge a path for themselves, being proud of what they do with no ill effects from residential schools. Every single child has my sincere hope for success! Their options for careers are possible for them now. I wish every First Nations child all the best. You will succeed as you should!

I will continue to speak publicly with my beautiful Elders group or when I get invites to schools or agencies. My message is: understand us, help us heal, and don't think so lowly of us because we are in trauma.

I feel we must break from the survivor mode, which suspends our lives in pain and agony with our bad memories. I know it is difficult and endless for you survivors, but we can heal ourselves with work and effort. We have to be patient, though, and move one step at a time. Be strong and resilient as you have been.

Perhaps the biggest and most positive change for me today is learning to respect and love myself and know that I can have merit in what I do today, even though this path has been so challenging for me. We deserve normalcy and peace. Sleep well and enjoy your lives as a people, especially with your families.

I will no longer lower my gaze. I will keep my head up as a proud First Nations man. I have no more guilt or shame! I love to recognize others out there, especially the beautiful Elders, as I am one now.

My story does not end here. I will continue to educate about residential schools, from my experiences. I would like the general public to change the perspective they have of our people and learn what we have been through as a people. We are in pain, as a people, from residential schools. As children, we endured so much trauma and live with painful memories. This is important to recognize.

It is there, embedded in the lives of our people. It may not be visible but we have pain, trauma and loss. My story is only one of 150,000 children but I am hopeful my input will show some of the horrors and treatment our children went through at residential schools across Canada for many decades.

Something that remains so eerie for me are the memories of residential schools I have visited over the years including Kuper Island, Port Alberni, Christie, Alert Bay, Sechelt, Williams Lake, Kamloops and St. Mary's. I just can't imagine all the pain that these places hold, as well the immense hardships these places brought to our people today. I know it has affected thousands of children and families.

We need to be proud of ourselves as a people again and help the young ones forge a path that will not be held back by experiences of generations before them. I know we have young ones who have empowering careers, who are breaking new paths into education. This is very important for our First Nations people, to see them move on to city councils, MLA or MP positions that show their capability as leaders. They will not be held back any longer and they function well in challenging areas across the lands, bringing the positive changes we need as a people. I am happy for them and proud of their efforts and accomplishments.

I know we will do well but it's vital we support each other and learn from each other as well. It is also imperative that we support each other to advance successes amongst our people. I feel we should no longer be held back or divided by colonial actions, laws and intentions.

One thing that comes to mind today are the words of our beautiful past Elders, who used to say, as I remember, "Things happen for a reason!" or "Keep your mind strong!" This is key for our people and youth now, as their potential is limitless and success can, and will be, a reality for them.

It shows that anything is possible, even though it may be challenging. They can reap the rewards and make changes for our people. They now blaze the trail for the young ones behind them. Remember, each of you can help them to succeed. Stand with them and give support to them as it's very important.

Perhaps for the intergenerational survivors, I feel it is important for you to make time to learn the stories of your family as it directly affects you. Even though you may not know it, you inherit much from your family. As we tend to pass on unhealthy actions and views we learned at residential schools, it is my feeling that our children and grandchildren should not have to carry our burdens any longer.

The impacts for me have been more than I thought, because of the abusive experiences I suffered. They affected my health, my body and mind, taking a large toll for a long time, which made me weak as a person and hindered so much of my life in everything I did daily. In some ways, I became developmentally delayed from the abuse from these brothers who were my supervisors at these residential schools. I was literally a bruised lost soul, indecisive and insecure within myself.

All the boundaries I lived with at the residential schools became a large part of my life. I unknowingly carried them with hardships most of the time. I was a very passive person, as I didn't want to rock the boat. We seem to hold much of it in, merely because we had to live there for years.

Today when I re-examine my life, I wonder how did this happen to me? It's unthinkable to reflect on most days because of what we endured there: pain, trauma and loss. Heartache of separation from family, community and culture. I know absolutely that I missed out on cultural events important to my family. I should have been there with them in our longhouse but I was at the residential school.

I am the poorer for not being able to stand with them during family cultural times. Now what hurts is not standing with my late grandfather Francis in our longhouse, to get my traditional family name. I did get the name later but not with him present.

I feel in my thoughts, we must remember all survivors out there who may have had hard times with losses of family and friends. They went to residential school and many have passed on to the spirit world. There was no one to talk to or turn to about the difficult times they encountered.

Our experiences will never leave our memories, ever, but we need to heal now as survivors and make the best of our time left here on this earth. It's very heartbreaking to remember, but it's time to let it go, my friends. We can cope with it now, and not let it be an issue in our lives any longer! We have never given up hope but our numbers dwindle every day. Continue to be strong my friends.

This colonial action of residential schools forever marks a difficult time across these lands for many survivors. Canada, along with the churches, worked together operating residential schools, taking so much from us. Please remember the last one closed a little over 25 years ago, 1996, and that is not very long ago, so it remains fresh amongst our people.

We must always remember this and not let them off the hook. Jointly, they brought us so much pain for which they must make amends to our people and survivors. No, we did not ask for this, but they boldly moved into creating residential schools for our people. They both must be held responsible and accountable!

I feel, personally, many survivors and communities have lost so much, their language, culture, family connections and close family members and more. Canada still has to address this in a fair fashion to restore what they took from us. Not with money, but programming and support. Please, not piecemeal funds either. They need to be sufficient to bring positive results.

I am hopeful you have learned something from the painful experiences that I shared. I have overcome these pains through sharing and talking about it. Believe me, they were tearful times for me ... anger, doubt, and questions about my predicament. My healing continues, making me stronger every day. My life has become more settled and firm for me now.

We survivors have to reclaim ourselves as a proud people, through counseling and sharing our stories and talking with other survivors. The young ones have to learn about the tragic times we had. I feel that their parents, grandparents and siblings still suffer quietly with trauma. They rarely share their painful times of residential experiences with anyone at all. Maybe they feel it is safer this way. But I feel it prolongs their hardships and difficulties. Be patient and love them as it's important.

I feel it is paramount for us to open ourselves to the therapy of our language, songs and art to move forward and be proud of what we get from the ancestors. Today I am so appreciative of those who sing proudly, drum and dance. They uplift my heart and make me proud. As it was the way of our people through history, I love to witness their passion, energy and love they have for the culture. It's important to nurture our spirits within us with culture and song, it shows we are a beautiful people.

Today I do not take anything lightly, especially the acknowledgements from people I don't know. On four different occasions young men approached me and introduced themselves, explaining who they are and where they were from. It is a part of our teaching. But I was very touched as I am now being recognized as an Elder. This meant so much to me. I am grateful for the nods I get from people out there. I cherish and relish it all! Of course, the smiles and hugs are always welcome too. As there are no barriers any longer for me as a person, my heart and arms are open.

Even though I had a hard time most of my life as a survivor, I want to love and cherish what time I have left on this earth. I don't want to be a bitter and angry old man; it's not my thing. Life is too short for this kind of situation to hold me in its grip.

Acknowledgements

My tower of strength is my wife Lorraine who has been by my side during some tough days that occurred in my life. We have been together as a couple for close to 50 years. Without her beside me I don't think I would be in this position today. Her support, love and understanding of me was huge, to make changes and move to what I do as a person today. I am grateful to her and have so much love for her for being with me when I had so much loss, such as my health struggles and forced retirement. I am eternally grateful to her as a supportive person, wife and friend.

My wife has suffered with her health for the last several years, along with many falls. We had tons of visits to emergency, logging many hospital hours. Eventually an MRI was done and it showed that she suffered a brain injury because of a fall to the ground. She had a buildup up of blood in her brain, which required immediate surgery to fix this problem that she was dealing with for a period of time.

Thankfully it went well with positive results and she is recovering. Support for her is vital as she stood by me with my hard times for years. It is my turn to be there for her and be the supportive one for her needs now. She also had a bout of thyroid cancer which was concerning for a couple of years. Eventually, she had surgery to remove the thyroid and had chemo treatment for it.

Her surgery and healing delayed my writing efforts for this book, but my relationship with my wife is important to me. For close to five decades, we shared our love and respect. We have had some challenges along the way, but we are still together and love one another.

Our youngest son had his Smart Car totally burn up. He barely escaped and it was traumatic for him. He just had seconds to get out of his vehicle before it was engulfed in flames. We are grateful he was not injured but he did lose a lot of equipment that day in his vehicle. He has recovered and is doing well today.

One morning, as I was making a fresh coffee with my French press, it slipped with hot boiling coffee. I was sprayed with scalding coffee on my face. It immediately began to blister and swell even beneath my hair. I was rushed to emergency in shock. Coffee grounds had to be flushed from my eyes, which were frozen first. Within days, most of my face turned black and my facial skin came off. It took a few weeks before new skin came back. Thankfully. More recently, we had flooding in our community and we were forced out of our home for a long period of time.

These events and hardships led to delays in completing my writing with the challenges faced by my family and me, I love and cherish them so much with all my heart. It is important for me personally to remember this, as we are all supportive of each other. This, of course, goes further and includes my siblings, nephews, nieces, grandchildren, cousins, many aunts and uncles I adore. I sincerely think of them all when I speak, as they had difficulties in the residential school as well, including intergenerational experiences for the young ones.

When I stand before people or groups, I address them using my Hul'qumi,num name, "Telexuts-sten," to proclaim my right as a First Nations person. This is who I am as a person. My traditional name goes back many generations in my family; it comes directly from my family roots. It was my late grandfather's name before me.

My traditional name makes me proud and honored today as a person. I do say my government name but sometimes forget. My name as a First Nations person will always connect me to my past, to generations of my ancestors. It makes me proud and strong. I thank Elder Mena from Cowichan and my nephew Chuck, for the spelling of my Hul'qumi'num name. It means so much to me. I lift my hands to you both in thanks for giving me the spelling of my ancestral name.

There are so many people in my life who have been instrumental in assisting me to become the person I am today with their words of support, hugs, and loving me in some tough times. I am grateful to you all, as one never knows how impactful you are when you interact with those in your lives. Small gestures or words mean so much to me. Many are connected to me in my writing; there are a lot for sure. I do appreciate your kind support or acknowledgement.

I have shared some of this writing with some dear friends who responded favorably. I felt I would not continue if my message didn't come through. They were so kind to me for reading my rough drafts. It has changed considerably since that time. They are Dr. Kelly Bannister, Dr. Nadine Cruickshanks and friend Iris Newman. I lift my hands up in thanks to you for supporting me. I send huge hugs of thanks to you all.

I am particularly thankful to Dr. Cruikshanks, who has heard me speak for years at Vancouver Island University. She read this manuscript and provided me some valuable input, to add or change my writing for clearer understanding. She also edited my writing. I was so weak at this part. She guided me along very well. Thanks Nadine.

Lorraine and myself, a picture of contentment taken by my son Kyle.

There were many more people who supported my writing to be published as a book, especially in the final year of raising funds, editing and publication. It is impossible to name everyone, but I am grateful to each one of you. In addition to my family and friends, Facebook friends from around the world encouraged me greatly. There were many donations to my Go Fund Me page that made it possible to pay for the publishing costs. Warren Goulding and Connie Manning of Askew Creek Publishing took great care with so many details to make sure the words and images looked great in book form, and to make it available for sale. Special thanks to Jodie Walsh, Laura Brandes, Kelly Bannister, Andrea Rondeau and Cicilia Ann Crocker who reviewed and gave comments to finalize the manuscript. Thanks also to the POLIS Project on Ecological Governance and the Centre for Global Studies for planning a special book launch event at the University of Victoria to share my story more widely.

My story is only one of many stories. My voice is only one of so many voices. Many of these stories can never be told because the voices have been silenced by trauma and by passing to the spirit world. I hope my voice and sharing my story can bring awareness to the stories of those who cannot speak for themselves today.

You Are Special

It's OK, open your eyes
Stand up and look around; your friends are gone
And much of your family

With flashing memories in your mind
With beautiful thoughts of bygone days
We shared together laughter, tears
Good times and bad

They are gone into the spirit world
But remembered and deeply loved
Remain treasured in our hearts

They are no longer in pain
Not suffering today
They want you to be happy
Don't be sad

Residential schools are gone
They no longer exist but in your heart
Breathe in and let it go

Heal your body and your mind
Find yourself and move on
As a proud First Nations person

Learn your history
Your language
Connections to the land and water
The sacred medicines

Your family, need you and your people too
Grandchildren look up to you
Needing your love and support

Love yourself! As you are special

–Raymond Tony Charlie

I was able to find the information below on the Internet. It has information about Doughty, our abuser, as well as others from residential school here in British Columbia. I am sharing from their online site. Kinney was a sex abuser at Kuper Island Residential School but not charged. No survivors came forth to charge him sadly. Probably because so few knew they were able to report him. The information I listed below about abusers may need to be updated but it was current at the time of my writing.

NATIVE INDIAN RESIDENTIAL SCHOOL ARREST – KINNEY EXTRADITED FROM THAILAND

March 2, 2007 – Gordon Irvin Kinney, aged 65, is back in Canada in police custody after being extradited from Thailand to stand trial on charges of sexual abuse arising out of the Native Indian Residential School Investigation.

Kinney was charged with three counts of indecent assault on a male and two counts of gross indecency in June 2002 as a result of incidents that occurred between 1964 and 1969 at the St. Mary's Native Residential School located in Mission B.C. Kinney could not be located and a Canada-wide warrant was issued for his arrest. Investigators were able to track Kinney to his new home in the Kingdom of Thailand and B.C. Crown counsel agreed to extradite him.

Kinney was arrested at his home in Chonburi, Thailand by members of the Royal Thai Police Immigration Unit on August 2, 2006, and has been in custody ever since. On December 14, 2006, a Thai Court ordered that Kinney be returned to Canada. Two members of the "E" Division of the Major Crime section flew to Bangkok, Thailand on February 25, 2007. Kinney was turned over to Canadian Police on March 2, 2007 and flown to Canada. He is currently in police custody and is scheduled to make his first appearance in Abbotsford Provincial Court at 9:30 a.m. on Monday, March 5, 2007.

Task Force investigators were able to determine that KINNEY left Canada in December 1999 and believed to be living in Thailand RCMP "E" Division Major Crime investigators, working with together with RCMP Liaison Officers in Bangkok and Kuala Lumpur, as well as Royal Thai Police and the Philippine National Police, were able to track Kinney down to an apartment complex in Chonburi, Thailand, which resulted in the 65-year-old man's arrest.

HISTORICAL BACKGROUNDER: RCMP NATIVE INDIANRESIDENTIAL SCHOOLS TASK FORCE

- The RCMP Native Indian Residential Schools Task Force was created in December 1994 to investigate complaints of historical physical and sexual abuse at the church-run residential schools around B.C.

- A total of 15 schools were under investigation

- The Task force investigated 974 separate offences. 515 were sexual offence involving 374 victims. Another 435 allegations of ; physical assault involving 223 victims (note: many of these victims were also the same victims of some of the sexual assault complaints. A total number of victims is not available)

- 33 per cent of all the suspects have deceased.

CHARGES LAID:

- To date, 14 individuals have been charged with offences in connections to Native Indian Residential Schools (includes charges laid prior to the creation of the Task Force)

- The only outstanding arrest is that of Edward FITZGERALD, Lejac Residential School. Charged with 21 sex and common assault related offences. He is believed to be in Ireland.

- Rev. HARDING, St. George's Residential School, Lytton. Acquitted at trial.

- Father McINTEE, Cariboo/St. Residential School. Convicted with sexual assault in 1989 and received 3 years in prison and 3 years probation.

- Bishop O'CONNOR, Cariboo/St. Joseph's Residential School. Charged in 1992. Appealed to Supreme Court of Canada twice. Charged were eventually stayed.

- Brother Glen DOUGHTY, Kuper Island Residential School and Cariboo/St. Joseph's. Charged and convicted on 3 separate occasions. Williams Lake in 1991- 12 months in jail. Nanaimo in 1995 – 4 months in jail and again in October 2002 – 3 years in jail.

- Jerzy MACZYNSKI, Lower Post Residential School. Convicted in early 1995- 16 years in jail. Died in Prison.

- Ben GARLAND, Lower Post Residential School. Convicted in early 1990s and died in prison.

- Arthur PLINT, Alberni Residential School. Convicted in 1995 and 1997. Currently serving an 11 – prison sentence.

- Gerald MORAN, St. Mary's Residential School, Mission. Convicted of several counts in New Westminster Supreme Court on September 7, 2004 and sentenced to 3 years in prison.

- Gordon KINNEY, St. Mary's Residential School, Mission. Charged with 8 counts.

- Donald HADDOCK, Alberni /Residential School, Port Alberni. Charged with 12 counts of sex-related offenses. Plead guilty Oct. 28, 2003. Sentenced to one year and 11 months in jail on Jan. 2004, followed by probation.

- Michael FLYNN, Alberni Residential School, Port Alberni. Charged with two counts of Indecent Assault on a male and count of Gross Indecency. Charges eventually stayed.

- David FORDE, Alberni Residential School, Port Alberni, Charged with four counts of Indecent Assault. He died in jail.

PHOTO CREDITS

- The photos used for this book were taken by myself from my personal collection; however, the rest were taken by other photographers which need to be credited.
- Photo of the 1917 Kuper Island Residential School was found online with no additional photo information.
- Photo of me at the TRC – Truth and Reconciliation event in Duncan was from the Cowichan newpaper.
- Photo of myself at the BC Ferries and Marine Workers Union convention in Vancouver was taken by Joshua Berson Photography.

CPSIA information can be obtained
at www.ICGtesting.com
Printed in the USA
LVHW080205260522
719797LV00013B/744